Eating out
en français

Eating out
en français

General Editor
Simon Collin

French Editor
Françoise Laurendeau

A & C Black • London

www.acblack.com

First published in Great Britain 2003

Reprinted 2005

A & C Black Publishers Ltd
37 Soho Square, London W1D 3QZ

© Bloomsbury Publishing Plc 2003
© A & C Black Publishers Ltd 2005

A CIP record for this book is available from
the British Library

ISBN 0-7136-7646-9

Text Production and Proofreading
Daisy Jackson

A & C Black uses paper produced with elemental
chlorine-free pulp, harvested from managed
sustainable forests.

Contents

Preface

If you have ever ordered from a menu written in French without being completely sure what you were asking for, then you need this pocket dictionary!

We have compiled this book to provide an essential pocket companion for any traveller who likes to know what they are ordering and eating. And unlike many other dictionaries, the text is fully bilingual — to and from English, so that you can easily translate a menu or ask for a favourite dish or a particular ingredient. We have included nearly 2,000 dishes and ingredients, with special chapters on wine and French cheeses (an essential part of any French meal).

This pocket book is structured in four main sections:

- English-French menu dictionary
- French-English menu dictionary
- French wines and wine terms
- French cheeses

The dictionary includes several pages of useful phrases. These have been selected to help you to find a restaurant, ask for the table that you want, order your meal, pay the bill — and, if necessary, complain.

We have also included helpful phrases for vegetarians, who traditionally have a difficult time eating out in France (where bacon and chicken are not always thought of as 'meat'!). Phrases to cover special diets are also included.

Finally, as you travel you will doubtless find new local dishes and local names for ingredients — in our experience, this is particularly so with local names for different types of fish. If you find interesting new terms that are not in this book, we would love to hear from you; please let us know and we will try and include the terms in future editions. Send any new terms (or comments on local variations of expressions) to: frenchfood@bloomsbury.com

Introduction

Types of restaurant

une auberge	*hotel-restaurant, usually in the country*
un bar	*serves alcoholic drinks*
un bistrot	*café-restaurant, serves drinks and simple meals*
une brasserie	*café-restaurant, choice of beer and simple meals*
un café	*serves alcoholic drinks and coffee, some serve ice cream*
un café-restaurant	*serves alcoholic drinks, serves meals*
une cafétéria	*self-service restaurant providing simple meals*
un restaurant	*proper dining*

	room; quality can vary
un restaurant d'autoroute	*motorway restaurant, often a cafeteria*
un restaurant gastronomique	*high quality food, though sometimes no choice of menu, often more expensive*
un salon de thé	*shop selling cakes with a few tables to have tea or coffee*

Closing times

As shops tend to shut abruptly for lunch, so, oddly, do some restaurants. Many smaller restaurants have a weekly closure timetable (fermeture hebdomadaire)— closing, commonly, on Sunday and Monday.

Tipping

Tipping is relatively straightforward: bills are often stamped 's.t.c.' (service, taxes, compris) and it means what it says—all service and taxes included. The only exception perhaps is to leave the small change in the saucer at a bar (if you are eating at the bar rather than at a table).

Public holidays in France (jours fériés)

New Year's Day
Easter Sunday and Monday
Labour Day, 1 May
VE Day, 8 May
Ascension Day
Whit Sunday and Monday
France's National Day (Bastille Day), 14 July
The Assumption, 15 August
All Saints' Day, 1 November
Armistice Day, 11 November
Christmas Day

Booking

If any of the national holidays above are part of your holiday, you should book well ahead for a place in a restaurant. Outside Paris, you should also book in advance for Sunday lunch, when large families settle down soon after mid-day to enjoy a long, noisy lunch. And don't imagine you can squeeze in for a second sitting: except for some Parisian or tourist-driven restaurants, there is no such thing.

Meals and eating times

07:00 — 09:00	petit déjeuner	*breakfast*
12:00 — 14:00	déjeuner	*lunch*
19:30 — 22:30	dîner	*dinner*

Restaurant rating schemes

Toques (chef's hats hats) (five toques = de luxe, one toque = fourth-class); Michelin stars (three-stars = exceptional, one-star = very good)

Useful French Phrases

Menu

Menus are usually split into five sections:

potage or hors-d' oeuvre	*soup or starter*
entrée	*first course*
plat principal	*main course*
fromage	*cheese course*
dessert	*dessert*

Shorter menus might have just three sections:

entrée	*first course*
plat principal	*main course*
dessert	*dessert*

Getting to a restaurant

Can you recommend restaurant?	*Quel restaurant nous recommandez -vous?*
I would like to reserve a table for this evening	*J'aimerais réserver une table pour ce soir*
Do you have a table for three/four people?	*Avez-vous une table pourtrois/quatre (personnes)?*
We would like the table for 8 o'clock	*Nous aimerions réserver unetable pour 20 heures*
Could we have a table ...?	*Auriez-vous une table de libre...?*
by the window	*près de la fenêtre*
outside	*dehors/à l'extérieur*
on the terrace	*sur la terrasse*
in the non-smoking area	*dans la section non-fumeurs*
in the smoking area	*dans la section fameurs*
What time do you open?	*A quelle heure ouvrez-vous?*
Could you order a taxi for me?	*Pourriez-vous me faire venir un taxi?*

RESTAURANT L'AUBERGE

Vous propose son menu gastronomique à €€34

Entrées

La terrine de canard aux pistaches
Le foie gras de canard confiture de figues
La soupe de peiswn et sa rouille
Le. Saumon mariné, à l'aneth

Poissons

Le filet de rouget au fenouil
La darne de saumon poêlée et mousse de brocoli Le St
Pierre poché aux poireaux et beurre blanc

Viandes

La fricassée de poulet à l'estragon
Le carrsé d'agneau persillé à l'ail
L'entrecôte grillée aux cèpes

Assiette de fromages

Le dessert de notre carte au choix

Lasalle à manger est non-fumeur

Prix nets — service compris

Chez Tante Claire

Menu Touristiq ue €18
service compris

Salade aux noix
ou
Potage du jour

———————

Magret de canard grillé
ou
Poulet fermier

———————

Frites
ou
haricots verts

———————

Fromage
ou
dessert

1/2 1. de vin et café compris

Ordering

Waiter/waitress!	*Monsieur! /Mademoiselle!*
What do you recommend?	*Que nous proposez-vous?*
What are the specials of the day?	*Quels sont les plats du jour?*
Is this the fixed-price menu?	*C'est le menu à prix fixe?*
Can we see the à-la-carte menu?	*Vous avez aussi un menu à la carte?*
Is this fresh?	*Est-ce frais?*
Is this local?	*Est-ce une spécialité de la région?*
I would like a/an ...	*J'aimerais un/une...*
Could I/we have ... please?	*Pourriez-vous me/nous donner...*
an ashtray	*un cendrier*
the bill	*l'addition*
our coats	*nos manteaux*
a cup	*une tasse*
a fork	*une fourchette*
a glass	*un verre*
a knife	*un couteau*
the menu	*le menu*
a napkin	*une serviette*

a plate	*une assiette*
a spoon	*une cuillère*
a toothpick	*un cure-den*
the wine list	*la carte des vins*
May I have some . . .?	*J'aimer ais avoir ...*
	Pourriez-vous
	m'apporter ...?
bread	*du pain*
butter	*du beurre*
ice	*de la glace*
(slice of) lemon	*une tranche de citron*
milk	*du lait*
pepper	*du poivre*
salt	*du sel*
sugar	*du sucre*
water	*de l'eau*
I would like it ...	*Je le/la préférerais*
	... Je l'aimerais ...
baked	*cuit(e) au four*
fried	*frit(e)*
grilled	*grillé(e)*
poached	*poché(e)*
smoked	*fumé(e)*
steamed	*(cuit(e)) à la vapeur*
boiled	*cuit(e) à l'eau/à*

	l'anglaise
roast	rôti(e)
very rare	bleu
rare	saignant(e)
medium	à point/rose
well-done	bien cuit(e)

V Useful phrases for vegetarians

I am ...	Je suis ...
vegetarian	végétarien (-ienne)
lacto-ovo-vegetarian	lacto-ovo-végétarien (-ienne)
lacto-vegetarian	lacto-végétarien (-ienne)
vegan	végétarien (-ienne)
I don't eat ...	Je ne mange pas
I don't eat meat, pork or chicken	Je ne mange pas ... de ne viande, de porc ou de poulet
I don't eat fish	Je ne mange pas de poisson
I eat eggs, milk and cheese	Je mange pas d'oeufs, de lait ou de fromage
I don't eat suet/lard/dripping	Je ne mange pas de suif/de saindoux/de graisse de viande
Do you have any	Avez-vous des plats

vegetarian dishes?	*végétariens?*
Is there a vegetarian restaurant near here?	*Y a-t-il un restaurant végétarien près d'ici?*
Is this cheese made with rennet?	*Ce fromage est-il fabriqué avec de la présure animale?*
Do you have a rennet-free cheese?	*Auriez-vous des fromages Sans présure?*
Do you serve this dish without meat/ eggs/cheese?	*Pourriez-vous préparer ce plat sans viande/oeufs/ fromage?*
Does this sauce/ soup contain beef/ chicken/fish/ meat stock?	*Est-ce que cette sauce/soupe contient du bouillon de boeuf/poulet/ poisson/viande?*
Does this dish contain gelatine/aspic?	*Est-ce que ce plat contient de la gélatine/de l'aspic?*
Does this contain organic ingredients?	*C'est bien un plat biologique?*
Do you use GM foods/MSG?	*Utilisez-vous des liments GMO/du glutamate de sodium?*

Useful phrases for people on special diets etc.

I am diabetic	*Je suis diabétique*
Does this dish contain nuts?	*Est-ce que ce plat contient des noix?*
I am allergic to ...	*Je suis allérgique à ...*
I have a peanut/ seafood/wheat allergy	*Je suis allergique à l'arachide/aux fruits demer/au blé*
I don't eat wheat/ gluten	Je ne mange pas de blé/degluten

Drinks

Can I see the wine list, please?	*Puis-je avoir la carte des vinss'ilvous plaît?*
I would like a/an ...	*J'aimerais* avoir ...
aperitif	*un apéritif*
another	*un deuxième; encore un(e)*
I would like a glass of...	*Puis-je avoir un verre de/d'...?*
red wine	*vin rouge*
white wine	*vin blanc*
rose wine	*vin rosé*

sparkling wine	*vin mousseux*
still water	*eau plate*
sparkling water	*eau gazeuse*
tap water	*eau du robinet*
With lemon	*avec du citron*
With ice	*avec de la glace*
With water	*avec de l'eau*
Neat	*sans eau ni glace*
I would like a bottle of...	*Donnez-moi une bouteille de ...*
this wine	*ce vin-ci*
house red	*de vin rouge maison*
house white	*de vin blanc maison*
Is this wine ...?	*Est-ce un vin ...?*
very dry	*très sec*
dry	*sec*
sweet	*doux/sucré*
local	*de la région*
This wine is ...	*Le vin ...*
not very good	*n'est pas très bon*
not very cold	*n'est pas très frais*
corked	*est bouchonné*
I would like a ...	*J'aimerais un/une ...*
fruit juice	*jus de fruits*
lemonade	*limonade*

non-alcoholic beer	*bière non alcoolisée*
non-alcoholic wine	*vin non alcoolisé*
low-alcohol beer	*bière peu alcoolisée*
low-alcohol wine	*vin peu alcoolisé*
non-alcoholic beverage	*boisson non alcoolisée*
decaffeinated coffee/tea	*thé/café décaféiné*
soft drink	*boisson non alcoolisée*

Complaints

This is not what I ordered	*Ce n'est pas ce que j'ai commandé*
I asked for...	*J'ai commandé ...*
Could I change this?	*Est-ce que je peux le changer pour autre chose?*
The meat is ...	*La viande ...*
overdone	*est trop cuite*
underdone	*n'est pas assez cuite*
tough	*est dure*
I don't like this	*Je n'aime pas ça*
The food is cold	*Tout est froid*
This is not fresh	*Ce n'est pas frais*
What is taking	*Pourquoi est-ce si*

23

| so long? | *long?* |
| This is not clean | *Ce n'est pas propre* |

Paying

Could I have the bill?	*Pourrez-vousm 'apportez l'addition?*
I would like to pay	*Gorçon, l'addition*
Can I charge it to my room?	*Vous l'ajoutez à ma note d'hôtel?*
We would like to pay seperately There's a mistake in the bill	*Chacun paye sa part Je crois qu 'il y a une erreursur la facture*
What's this amount for?	*Ce montant représente quoi?*
Is service included?	*Le service est-il compris?*
Do you accept traveller's cheques?	*Acceptez-vous les chèques devoyage?*
Can I pay by credit card?	*Vous acceptz les cartes decrédit?*

Numbers

0	*zéro*	15	*quinze*
1	*un(e)*	16	*seize*
2	*deux*	17	*dix-sept*
3	*trois*	18	*dix-huit*
4	*quatre*	19	*dix-neuf*

5	*cinq*	20	*vingt*
6	*six*	30	*trente*
7	*sept*	40	*quarante*
8	*huit*	50	*cinquante*
9	*neuf*	60	*soixante*
10	*dix*	70	*soixante-dix*
11	*onze*	80	*quatre-vingt(s)*
12	*douze*	90	*quatre-vingt-dix*
13	*treize*	100	*cent*
14	*quatorze*	200 etc.	*deux cents etc.*

French-English

Aa

abats giblets
abattis *[de volaille]* giblets
abricot apricot
absinthe absinthe
accompagnement *[garniture]* trimmings
acide sharp
addition bill, *[US]* check
agneau lamb
agrumes citrus
aiglefin haddock
    aiglefin fumé *[haddock]* smoked
    haddock
aïgo bouido Provençal garlic soup served
  over pieces of bread
aigre sour
aigre-doux (-douce) sweet and sour
aiguillat dogfish
ail garlic
    aillé(e) garlicky
ailloli, aïoli garlic-flavoured mayonnaise
airelle blueberry
airelle rouge small cranberry
algue seaweed
aligot de Lozère potato, cheese and garlic
  purée

28

alimentation   small shop selling general groceries

allumettes   matches
  allumettes au fromage   (fine) cheese straws
  pommes allumettes   matchstick potatoes

alose   shad

alouette   lark *[bird]*
  alouette sans tête   beef olive

aloyau *[faux-filet]* sirloin

amande (douce)   almond
  aux amandes   with almonds
  pâte d'amandes   almond paste

amandine   almond tart

amer (amère)   bitter

américaine, sauce   the cooking liquor from lobster mixed with the lobster coral and cream

amoricaine, à l'   with brandy, white wine, onions, and tomatoes

amuse-gueule *[hors-d'oeuvre]* hors-d'oeuvre; *[US]* appetizer

ananas   pineapple

anchois   anchovy
  anchoïade   anchovy dipping sauce
  anchois de Norvège   sprat

andouille, andouillette   sausage made of chitterlings, pork meat, onions, seasoning, etc.

French-English

aneth   dill

ange de mer   angel fish

anglaise, à l'   plain boiled *[vegetables]*

anglaise, sauce   see **crème à l'anglaise**

anglaise, sauce à l'   thin crème à
l'anglaise sauce

angélique   angelica

anguille   eel

   anguille fumée   smoked eel

anis   aniseed

anone *[pomme canelle]*   custard apple

apéritif   aperitif

arachide   peanut

arêtes (de poisson)   (fish) bones

aromatisé   flavoured

arôme (d'un vin)   bouquet

arrow-root   arrowroot

artichaut   artichoke

   fond d'artichaut   artichoke heart

asperge   asparagus

   pointes d'asperges   asparagus tips

aspic   aspic

assaisonné   seasoned

assaisonnement   seasoning

assiette   plate

   **assiette anglaise, assiette de viandes
   froides**   assorted cold
   meat; *[US]* cold cuts

   assiette de viandes grillées   mixed grill

aubergine   aubergine; *[US]* eggplant

au gratin   with a topping of cheese and breadcrumbs

aumônière   pouch-shaped pancake filled with fruit salad, ice cream, etc.

autruche   ostrich

aveline   filbert

avocat   avocado

    avocat gratiné au four   baked avocado gratin

    avocats gratinés au parmesan   baked avocado and cheese gratin

avoine   oats

Bb

baba au rhum   rum baba

bacon   bacon

baguette *[pain]*   French bread

baguettes *[chinoises]*   chopsticks

ballottine   faggot

bambou   bamboo

banane   banana

    bananes flambées   banana flambé

    banane verte *[plantain]*   plantain

bar *[loup de mer]*   sea bass

barbue   brill

bardane burdock

barquette small tart *[shaped like a boat]*

basilic basil

basquaise, à la Basque style, with ham, red peppers, tomatoes

bâtonnets batons *[of carrots, etc.]*

baudroie *[lotte de mer]* monkfish

bavarois Bavarian cream

bavette flank (of beef)

bavette, bavoir (child's) bib

bayonnaise, à la braised in Madeira wine

béarnaise, sauce hollandaise sauce but thicker and with tarragon.
Served warm with grilled meat and fish

bécasse woodcock

bécassine snipe

béchamel, sauce béchamel a basic whitesauce made frombutter, flour and seasoned milk

beignet *[pâte frite et sucrée]* doughnut,fritter

> **beignet viennois** doughnut
> **beignet fourré à la confiture** jam doughnut
> **beignet de bananes** banana fritter
> **beignets de légumes** vegetable fritters
> **beignet de pommes** apple fritter

belon type of oyster from Brittany

Bercy, sauce chopped shallots cooked in butter with white wine and fish stock added

bergamote bergamot
bette chard
betterave beetroot
    betteraves rouges à la crême
    creamed beetroot
beurre butter
    avec (du) beurre; au beurre with butter
    sans beurre without butter
    beurre blanc sauce of white wine,
    vinegar, shallots, butter
    beurre clarifié *[cuisine indienne]* ghee
    beurre d'anchois anchovy butter
    beurre de cacah(o)uètes/d'arachides
    peanut butter
    beurre de cacao cocoa butter
    beurre de truffes truffle butter
    beurre fondu melted butter
    beurre noir browned melted butter
    with vinegar and seasoning
    beurre noisette brown butter
    beurre sans sel unsalted butter
bien cuit(e) well done
bière beer
    bière (à la) pression draught beer
    bière anglaise blonde ale
    bière anglaise pression bitter (beer)
    bière blonde lager
bifteck steak; *[US]* beefsteak
bigarade, sauce sauce made from the
  remains of duck with Seville orange and
  lemon juice

French-English

French-English

bigorneau   winkle
biologique   organic
biscotte   crispbread, rusk
biscuits *[gâteaux secs]*   biscuits; *[US]*
  cookies
    biscuits a la cuillere   sponge fingers
bisque de homard   lobster bisque
blanc d'oeuf   egg white
blanchaille   whitebait
blanchir   to blanch
blanc-manger   blancmange
blanquette de veau   veal stew in cream
  sauce
blé   wheat
    blé concassé bulgur wheat, bulgar wheat
    blé noir *[sarrasin]*   buckwheat
blennie   butterfish
blette   chard
blinis   blinis
boeuf   beef
    boeuf (à la) bourguignonne   see
    bourguignonne
    boeuf de conserve   corned beef
    boeuf en daube   beef casserole
    boeuf stroganoff   beef stroganoff
    rôti de boeuf *[rosbif]*   roast beef
boisson   drink
boisson (gazeuse) non alcoolisée   soft
  drink
boîte (de conserve)   tin; *[US]* can
    en boîte   tinned; *[US]* canned

bol   bowl
bombe   bombe
bonbon   sweet; *[US]* candy
bonne femme   cooked with leeks and
  potatoes
bonite   bonito; skipjack tuna
bordeaux rouge   claret, red Bordeaux
bordelaise, à la   with red wine, bone
  marrow, mushrooms and artichokes
bouchée (feuilletée)   vol au vent
    bouchée à la reine   chicken vol au vent
boucherie chevaline   butcher's selling
  horsemeat
boudin blanc   sausage of finely ground
  white meat
boudin noir   black pudding
bouillabaisse   Provençale fish stew
bouillir   to boil
bouilli(e) *[cuit(e)* à *l'eau,* à *l'anglaise]*
  boiled
bouillon   broth, stock
    bouillon de boeuf beef stock, beef
    broth
    bouillon de légumes   vegetable stock
    bouillon végétarian   vegetable stock
boulangerie   bakery
boule   flat round loaf with coarse crust
boulede glace   scoop of ice cream
boules de picoulat   Catalan dish of pork
  meatballs in a bean casserole
boulette de pâte   dumpling

boulette de viande meat ball
bouquet garni bouquet garni *[mixed herbs]*
bouquet *[crevette rose]* prawn
bourgeoise, à la cooked in family style
bourguignonne, à la with red wine, mushrooms, small onions and bacon
bourrache borage
bourride Provençale fish dish with garlic mayonnaise
bouteille bottle
>**bouteille d'eau (minérale)** bottle of (mineral) water
>**bouteille de vin** bottle of wine

braisé(e) braised
braiser to braise
branche stick, stalk
brandade de morue salt cod purée
brasserie café-restaurant serving simple meals and beer; brewery
brebis ewe
brème bream
brème de mer sea bream
brési air-dried beef from Franche-Comté
brik North African pasty filled with egg, tuna and vegetables
brioche brioche
Brocciu Corsican cream cheese made with sheep or goat's milk
broche, à la grilled on a skewer over a flame

brochet pike
brochette skewer
brocolis broccoli
brugnon *[nectarine]* nectarine
brûlé(e) burnt
bruler to burn
brune, sauce *see* **demi-glace**
buccin whelk
buche de Noël Christmas log
buffet buffet

Cc

cabécou goat's or ewe's milk cheese, often served warm
cabillaud (fresh) cod
cacah(o)uète peanut
cacao cocoa, chocolate
café coffee
    café au lait coffee with milk
    café complet continental breakfast
    café crème, un crème (large) coffee with cream or milk
    café décaféiné decaffeinated coffee; decaf
    café express espresso, expresso coffee

café filire   filter coffee
café instantane   instant coffee
café liègoise   iced coffee served with cream or whipped cream
café noir black coffee
café soluble   instant coffee
petit crème   (small) coffee with cream of milk
caféine   caffeine
sans caféine *[décaféiné]* caffeine-free, decaffeinated
cafetière   coffee pot
caille   quail
oeufs de caille   quails' eggs
cake   fruit cake
calmar *[encornet]* squid
camomille *[infusion de, tisane de]* camomile (tea)
canapés   canapés
canard   duck *[domestic]*
canard (à la) rouennaise   duck stuffed with its own liver, in a red wine sauce
canard à l'orange   duck with oranges
canard de Barbaric   Barbary duck
canard sauvage   wild duck
caneton   duckling
canette   duckling *[female]*
canneberge   cranberry
cannelle   cinnamon
cannelloni   cannelloni

cannelloni aux champignons
mushroom cannelloni

cantaloup cantaloup (melon)

cappuccino cappuccino coffee

câpres capers

carafe carafe

   carafe d'eau carafe of water, jug of water

caramel caramel

   caramel (au beurre) toffee

carbon(n)ade de boeuf beef braised with onions and beer

cardamome cardamom

cari curry

carotte carrot

   carottes Vichy carrots stewed in butter, sugar and seasoning

carpaccio wafer-thin slices of raw beef or tuna

carpe carp

carré rack

   carré *[d'agneau, de porc, etc.]* rack of ribs

   carré d'agneau rack of lamb

carrelet plaice

carte menu

   carte, à la each menu item is priced separately

carte des vins wine list

carthame safflower

cartilage *[croquant]* gristle

French-English

carvi caraway
casher kosher
cassate cassata
casserole casserole
cassis blackcurrant
cassoulet casserole from Languedoc, with haricot beans, pork, sausage or goose
    cassoulet végétarian vegetarian bean casserole
catalane, à la with tomatoes, black olives and garlic
cavaillon honeydew melon
caviar caviar
    caviar d'aubergine pureed roasted aubergines
cédrat citron
céleri celery
céleri-rave celeriac
céndrier ashtray
cèpe cep; porcini mushroom
céréales (froides) (breakfast) cereal
cerfeuil chervil
cerise cherry
    cerise confite glacé cherry
    cerise noire black cherry
cervelas saveloy
cervelle brains
    cervelle de veau calf's brains
chaise chair
chambré(e) at room temperature
champagne champagne

French-English

champignon mushroom
    champignons de Paris button mushrooms
    champignons farcis stuffed mushrooms
chandelier candlestick
chandelle candle
chanterelle chanterelle *[mushroom]*
Chantilly (with) whipped cream
chapelure breadcrumbs
chapon capon
charbon de bois charcoal
charlotte charlotte
    charlotte aux pommes apple charlotte
chasseur, sauce red wine boiled with shallots, garlic, mushrooms, tomatoes and demi-glace sauce
châtaigne sweet chestnut
    châtaigne d'eau water chestnut
Chateaubriand, chateaubriant Chateaubriand *[thick piece of grilled fillet of beef]*
chaud(e) hot *[not cold]*
chaud-froid jelly, aspic *[savoury]*
    chaud-froid de poulet chicken in jelly, aspic of chicken
chaudrée chowder
(faire) chauffer to heat up
chausson turnover
    chausson aux pommes apple turnover

French-English

chef chef, cook
cherry brandy *[liqueur de cerise]* cherry brandy
cheval horsemeat
cheveux d'ange angel hair (pasta)
chèvre goat
chèvres en papillote goats cheese filo parcels
chevreuil venison *[deer]*
    chevreuil *[à la scandinave]* reindeer
chicorée frisée endive, frisée salad
chien de mer dogfish
chili con carne *[plat mexicain]* chilli con carne
    chili végétarien vegetable chilli
chinchard horse mackerel
chips (potato) crisps; *[US]* chips
chocolat chocolate, cocoa
    chocolat au lait milk chocolate
    chocolat blanc white chocolate
    chocolat glacé chocolate-covered ice lolly
    chocolat noir dark chocolate
    un chocolat *[bonbon]* a chocolate *[sweet]*
    un chocolat *[une tasse]* a cup of cocoa/hot chocolate
choix choice
    au choix, choix de choice of
    choix de légumes assorted vegetables

chou cabbage
  chou blanc white cabbage
  chou de Chine Chinese cabbage
  chou rouge red cabbage
  chou vert *[pommé]* green cabbage
  chou vert frisée *[non pommé]* kale
  chou vert frisée *[pommé]* savoy
  cabbage
chou à la crème cream puff
choucroute pickled cabbage
chou-fleur cauliflower
  chou-fleur sauce Mornay, au gratin
  cauliflower cheese
chou-navet swede
chou-rave kohlrabi
choux de Bruxelles Brussels sprouts
ciboule spring onion; *[US]* scallion
ciboulette chives
cidre (de pomme) cider
  cidre de poire perry *[pear cider]*
cigarettes russes sweet rolled crisp
  wafer filled with hazelnut cream
citron lemon
  citron pressé freshly squeezed lemon
  juice drunk diluted with water and
  sugar
  citron vert *[lime]* lime
citronnelle lemon grass
cive spring onion; *[US] scallion*
civet stew of rabbit, hare or other game
  civet de lièvre jugged hare

43

civette chives
clafoutis aux cérises cherries baked in a
 thick batter
claire type of oyster
clémentine clementine
climatisé(e) air-conditioned
clou de girofle clove
clovisse clam
cochon de lait suck(l)ing pig
coeur heart
coeur à la crème curd cheese dessert
 made in heart-shaped mould
coeur d'artichaut artichoke heart
cognac brandy
coing quince
colin *[merlu]* hake
colin *[lieu noir]* saithe
colvert mallard
compote de fruits stewed fruit
compris(e) included
compte account
concombre cucumber
condiment condiment
confiserie shop selling handmade
 chocolates, sweets and cakes
confit de canard/d'oie duck/goose
 preserved in own fat
confit(e) *[fruit, etc.]* candied
confiture jam
  confiture de fraises strawberry jam

confiture d'oranges (orange) marmalade

congelés frozen foods

congre *[anguille de mer]* conger eel

conserves preserves

consommé clear soup, consommé (soup)

   consommé froid cold consommé

   consommé en tasse/en gelée jellied consommé

   contrefilet sirloin steak

coq au vin chicken cooked in red wine

coque, à la soft-boiled *[egg]*

coques cockles

coquetier egg cup

coquillages shellfish

coquille St Jacques scallop

coriandre coriander

cornet (de glace) *[ice cream]* cone, cornet

cornichon gherkin

   cornichon saumuré/au vinaigre pickled gherkin

côte chop

   côte de porc pork chop

côtelette cutlet, chop

   côtelette d'agneau lamb chop

côtes ribs

   côtes de boeuf ribs of beef

cotriade Breton fish stew with onions, potato and cream

coulibiac   fish pie stuffed with rice and hard-boiled egg

coulis   coulis *[sauce of sieved puréed fruit]*

coupe glacée   dish of ice cream; sundae

couper   to cut

courge   squash, marrow *[vegetable]*

courgette   courgette; *[US]* zucchini

    courgettes farcies   stuffed courgettes

court-bouillon   fish stock

couscous   couscous

couteau   knife

couvert   cutlery

crabe *[tourteau]*   crab

    crabe décortiqué   prepared crab

    crabe froid à l'anglaise/à la russe dressed crab

crème   cream

    crème légèré/épaisse   single/double creamream

    à la crème   with cream; with cream sauce

    crème aigre   sour cream

    crème (à l') anglaise   thick egg custard made from egg yolks and milk

    crème au beurre   butter cream *[filling for cake]*

    crème caramel   creme caramel *[baked custard with caramel sauce]*

    crème Chantilly, crème fouettée whipped cream

French-English

crabe froid à l'anglaise/à la russe
dressed crab

crème cream

    crème légèré/épaisse single/double creamream

    à la crème with cream; with cream sauce

    crème aigre sour cream

    crème (à l') anglaise thick egg custard made from egg yolks and milk

    crème au beurre butter cream *[filling for cake]*

    crème caramel creme caramel *[baked custard with caramel sauce]*

    crème Chantilly, crème fouettée whipped cream

    crème fleurette top of the milk; single cream

    crème fraîche creme fraîche *[soured double cream]*

    crème pâtissière confectioner's custard

un crème, un café crème a (large) coffee with cream or milk

crème (de) *[velouté]* cream of

    crème d'asperges cream of asparagus soup

    crème de tomates cream of tomato soup

    crème de volaille cream of chicken soup

crémeux (-euse) creamy

crème fleurette   top of the milk; single cream

crème fraîche   creme fraîche *[soured double cream]*

crème pâtissière   confectioner's custard

un crème, un café crème   a (large) coffee with cream or milk

crème (de) *[velouté]*   cream of

crème d'asperges   cream of asparagus soup

crème de tomates   cream of tomato soup

crème de volaille   cream of chicken soup

crémeux (-euse)   creamy

créole   *[savoury]* with rice, tomatoes, pepper; *[sweet]* with orange peel

crêpe   pancake

crêpes gratinées   stuffed pancakes with cheese topping

cresson   cress

cresson de fontaine   watercress

crevette (grise)   shrimp

crevette rose   king prawn

crevettes mayonnaise   shrimp cocktail

croissant   croissant

croissant au beurre   croissant made with butter

croque-madame   fried cheese and ham sandwich topped wi th a fried egg

croquembouche pyramid of profiteroles
with caramel, served at weddings
croque-monsieur fried cheese and ham
sandwich
croquette de poisson fish cake
   croquettes de pommes de terre
   potato croquettes
crottin de chèvre small round goat's cheese
croustade bread or pastry case
croustillant crisp
croûte fried or toasted bread base
croûtons croutons
crudités raw sliced vegetables as an hors
d-oeuvre
cru(e) raw, uncooked
crumble crumble
crustacés shellfish
cube: en cubes diced [cubed]
cuillère, cuiller spoon
      cuillère à café coffee spoon
      cuillère à dessert tablespoon
      cuillère à soupe soup spoon
      cuillère à thé teaspoon
cuisine cookery, cooking
      cuisine bourgeoise plain home cooking
      cuisine maigre low-fat cooking
      cuisine nouvelles nouvelle cuisine
      cuisine régionale regional cooking
      cuisine végétarienne vegetarian
      cooking

French-English

cuisses de grenouilles frog's legs
cuissot haunch **cuit(e)** cooked, done
    cuit(e) au four baked
    cuit(e) à grande friture deep-fried
    cuit(e) à la vapeur steamed
    pas assez cuit(e) underdone
    trop cuit(e) overdone
cumin cumin (seed)
    cumin des prés caraway (seeds)
curcuma turmeric
cure-dent(s) toothpick
curry curry

Dd

dacquoise meringue filled with cream and soft fruit
dame blanche chocolate sundae with Chantilly
darne de saumon salmon steak
datte date
daube rich casserole of meat, vegetables, garlic, herbs, and red wine
daurade bream
dé: en dés diced, cubed, chopped
déca decaf
    un déca a decaf coffee

décaféiné   decaffeinated
  café décaféiné   decaffeinated coffee
découper   to carve
défense de fumer   no smoking
dégeler   to thaw
déglacer   to deglaze *[mix meat juices at bottom of pan with stock or wine]*
dégustation   tasting
déguster   to taste, to savour
déjeuner *[lunch]* lunch; to have lunch
délicieux (-euse)   delicious
demi   half
demi-bouteille   halfbottle
demi-glace, sauce   a mixture of equal parts of espagnole sauce and
brown stock reduced, used as a basis for other sauces
désossé(e) *[en filets]* filleted
désossé(e) *[sans os, sans arête]* boned
désosser *[lever les filets]* to fillet; *[enlever les os, les arêtes]* to debone
dessert   dessert
desservir (la table)   to clear up
diable (à la)   devilled
    rognons à la (sauce) diable   devilled kidneys
    diable, sauce   a sauce of chopped shallots, white wine, vinegar, cayenne pepper and coarsely ground white pepper. Served with fried or grilled fish or meat

dijonnaise, à la with mustard, or blackcurrants

dinde turkey
    dinde rôtie roast turkey

dîner *[midi]* lunch

dîner *[soir]* dinner, supper

dorade (aux sourcils d'or) gilthead bream

dorée *[poisson]* John Dory

dorer, faire dorer to brown

dormeur *[tourteau]* crab

dragées sugared almonds

Dubarry, à la with cauliflower

duchesse piped potato mixed with egg yolk

dur(e) hard-boiled; *[meat]* tough

duxelles, sauce white wine, mushrooms and shallots mixed with demi-glace sauce and tomato purée

Ee

eau water
    eau de seltz soda water
    eau de source spring water
    eau de vie fruit or nut brandy
    eau en bouteille bottled water

eau gazeuse sparkling water, fizzy water
eau glacée/très froide iced water
eau minérale mineral water
eau plate still (mineral) water
sans eau ni glace neat; *[US]* straight *[whisky, etc.]*
eau de vie de prunelle sloe gin
ébréché(e) *[verre, assiette]* chipped (glass, plate)
échalote shallot
éclair éclair
   éclair au chocolat chocolate eclair
écorce (de citron, etc.) (lemon, etc.) peel
   écorce confite candied peel
   écorce râpée *[zeste]* grated peel, zest
écrevisse crayfish
édulcorant sweetener
églefin haddock
émincés de veau/volaille thinly sliced cooked veal/chicken, served in a sauce
endive chicory
enrobé de coated with
entrecôte rib steak of beef
   entrecôte à la bordelaise rib steak cooked in sauce made of Bordeaux wine, butter, herbs, shallots, bone marrow
entrée starter
entremets salé savoury

épaule *[palette]* shoulder
éperlan   smelt
épice spice
épicé(e) spicy
épinard   spinach
   épinards en purée   creamed spinach
éplucher to peel escalope escalope
   escalope de dinde   turkey escalope
   escalope de veau   veal escalope
escargot   snail
espagnole, sauce   sauce made from
   browned flour and butter mixed with
   tomato purée and brown stock flavoured
   with browned vegetables
espadon   swordfish
Esquimau®   ice lolly
estragon   tarragon
esturgeon   sturgeon
express espresso

Ff

faînes   beech nuts
faisan   pheasant
faisselle   curd cheese

falafel   falafel
far breton   Breton speciality of prune
  shortcake
farce   stuffing
farci(e)   stuffed (with)
farine   flour
    farine d'avoine   oatmeal
    farine de châtaigne   chestnut flour
    farine de maïs   cornmeal, polenta
faux filet   sirloin steak
fécule de maïs   cornflour
fenouil   fennel
fermier *[oeuf, poulet]* free range, farm
  [egg, chicken]
fermière   with carrots, turnip, onion,
  celery
feuille de laurier   bay leaf
feuilles de vigne   vine leaves
feuilleté   sweet or savoury puff pasty
    feuilleté au fromage   puff pastry with
    cheese filling
fève   bean
    fève des marais, grosse fève   broad
    bean
fiadone   Corsican lemon-flavoured
  cheesecake
ficelle   French bread *[very long thin loaf]*
ficelle picarde   ham rolled in pancake
  served with white sauce
figue   fig
filet   fillet; tenderloin

filet de porc   pork tenderloin

filet de boeuf fillet of beef; *[US]* beef tenderloin

filet de boeuf en croûte beef Wellington

filet mignon   steak cut from end of fillet

filet de volaille   breast of chicken or turkey

fines herbes   mixed herbs

flageolet   flageolet (beans)

flambé(e)   flambé

flamiche   northern French sweet or savoury pastry tart

flan   baked custard

flet   flounder

flétan   halibut

flétan noir black halibut, Greenland halibut

flocons   flakes

flocons d'avoine rolled oats

florentine with spinach

foie liver

foies de poulets/de volaille   chicken livers

foie de veau   calf's liver

foie d'oie, foie gras   goose liver pâté

fondant *[sweet]* fondant

fondant au chocolat chocolate fudge (icing)

fondant *[meat, vegetables]* tender

fondue fondue
> **fondue bourguignonne** meat fondue
> **fondue savoyarde** cheese fondue

forestière with mushrooms, bacon, sauté potatoes

forêt-noire Black Forest gateau

forfait boissons drinks included

formule menu option

fougasse Provençal flat bread

four oven
> **cuit(e) au four** baked
> **pommes au four** baked apples

fourchette fork

fourré(e) (à/au/aux) filled (with), stuffed (with)

frais (fraîche) fresh

fraise strawberry
> **fraise des bois, fraise sauvage** wild strawberry
> **glace à la fraise** strawberry ice cream

framboise raspberry

frangipane rich pastry cream filling made with ground almonds

friand puffed pastry filled with meat
> **friand a la saucisse** sausage roll
> **friand au jambon** ham roll *[in puffed pastry]*

fricandeau braised veal

fricassée stew
> **fricassée de boeuf** stewed steak, beef stew

frisée aux noix curly endive salad with walnuts

frire to fry

frit(e) fried

frites (potato) chips; *[US]* French fries

friture de poissons mixed fried fish

froid(e) cold

fromage cheese

    fromage 'cottage' cottage cheese

    fromage à la crème cream cheese

    fromage à pâte dure hard cheese

    fromage à pâte molle soft cheese

    fromage blanc creamy low-fat cow's milk cheese

    fromage bleu blue cheese

    fromage de (lait de) brebis sheep's milk cheese

    fromage de chèvre goat's cheese

    fromage de lait entier full-fat cheese

    fromage frais soft cow's milk cheese, often with added cream

    plateau à fromage, plateau à de fromages cheese board

fromage de tête brawn

froment wheat

fruit fruit

    fruits confits crystallised fruit

    fruits frais fresh fruit

    fruits de mer seafood, shellfish

fumé(e) smoked, cured

French-English

Gg

galantine galantine
galette pancake
    galette de pommes de terre potato pancake
    galette de sarrasin buckwheat pancake
galette des Rois Twelfth Night cake *[round puff pastry cake with almond paste filling]*
garbure thick vegetable soup of cabbage, beans, potatoes, leeks, ham, herbs, etc.
garçon waiter
garni with vegetables
garniture filling; garnish; serving of vegetables
gaspacho gazpacho
gâteau cake, gateau
    gâteau à la crème cream cake
    gâteau au fromage blanc cheesecake
    gâteau au gingembre ginger cake
    gâteau aux carottes carrot cake
    gâteau de Noël *[anglais]* Christmas cake
    gâteau de Pithiviers round puff or flaky pastry tart filled with almond paste

gâteau de Savoie madeira cake
gâteau mousseline sponge cake
gâteau quatre-quarts pound cake
gâteau renversé upside-down cake
gâteau roulé swiss roll
gâteaux secs biscuits; *[US]* cookies
gaufre de miel honeycomb
gaufres waffles
gaufrette wafer
gélatine gelatine
gelée jelly
gelée à la menthe mint jelly
gelée de groseilles redcurrant jelly
genièvre *[eau-de-vie]* gin
baie de genièvre juniper berry
génoise sponge cake
génoise au citron madeira cake
germe de blé wheatgerm
germes de luzerne alfafa sprouts
germes de soja bean sprouts
gésiers gizzards
gibier (à plume/à poil) game
gigot d'agneau leg of lamb
gingembre ginger
gîte à la noix silverside
glaçage icing
glace ice
avec glace with ice; *[whisky, etc.]*
with ice, on the rocks
sans eau ni glace neat; *[US]* straight
[whisky, etc.]

glace *[crème glacée]* ice cream
    glace à la vanille   vanilla ice cream
glace *[pour gâteaux]* icing
glacé(e) *[very cold]* icy cold
glacé(e) *[de sucre, etc.]* glazed
glaçon   ice cube
glouteron   burdock
glucides *[hydrates de carbone]*
  carbohydrate
glutamate monosodique/de sodium
  monosodium glutamate (MSG)
gluten   gluten
    sans gluten   gluten free
gnocchi Parmentier potato dumplings
gombo   gumbo, okra, ladies finger
gougère   choux pastry ring with added
  cheese
goujon *[poisson]* gudgeon
    goujons de poulet   goujons, strips of
    fried fish or chicken
goulash, goulasch   goulash
gousse d'ail   garlic clove
gousse de vanille vanilla pod/bean
goyave   guava
grain   grain
    grains de genièvre juniper berries
    grains de raisin   grapes
graine   seed
    graines de pavot poppy seeds
    graines de sésame   sesame seeds
granité   sorbet; granita

gras fat *[noun]*
> **qui contient peu de gras** low in fat

gras (grasse) fat *[adj]*

gras-double tripe

gratin dauphinois scalloped potatoes cooked with cream

gratiné(e) browned; *[US]* au gratin

grenade pomegranate

grenadine grenadine

gribiche, sauce mashed hard-boiled egg yolks blended with oil and vinegar, flavoured with capers and gherkins, tarragon, chervil and parsley

gril grill *[noun]*

grillade grilled piece of meat
> **grillade de veau** grilled veal chop

grillé(e) grilled
> **grillé(e) au barbecue** barbecued
> **grillé(e) au charbon de bois** charcoal-grilled

griller to grill

grive thrush

grondin gurnard

groseille à maquereau gooseberry
> **groseille rouge** redcurrant

gros sel rock salt

grosse fève broad bean and sweet pepper salad

grouse grouse

guimauve marshmallow

Hh

hachis *[viande hachée]* minced meat
    hachis de boeuf minced beef; *[US]* ground beef
    hachis Parmentier shepherd's pie
haddock *[aiglefin fumé]* smoked haddock
hamburger hamburger
    hamburger végétal veggie burger
hareng herring
    hareng mariné pickled herring
    hareng saur/fumé kipper
    hareng roulé (mariné) rollmop (herring)
harenguet sprat
haricot bean
    haricots blancs haricot beans
    haricots blancs aux tomates baked beans
    haricots grimpants runner beans
    haricots noirs black beans
    haricots rouges kidney beans, red beans
    haricots verts green beans, French beans
harissa hot chilli paste served with couscous
heure du thé tea-time

hochepot Belgian thick soup of pork, beef, mutton, cabbage and other vegetables

hollandaise, sauce thick sauce made from egg yolks, a little pepper and vinegar, whisked over a gentle heat

homard lobster

hongroise, à la with paprika and fresh cream

houmous hummus

hors d'oeuvre hors d'oeuvre; [US] appetizer

hot dog [saucisse de Francfort dans un petit pain] hot dog

huile oil

    à l'huile with oil

    huile d'arachide peanut oil, groundnut oil

    huile de tournesol sunflower oil

    huile de noix walnut oil

    huile d'olive olive oil

    huile d'olive vierge virgin olive oil

    huile de pépins de raisin grapeseed oil

huître oyster

hydromel mead

hyposodé(e) low-salt

Ii

igname yam
îles flottantes floating islands *[dessert of poached egg whites in custard]*
incorporer to blend; to mix
indienne, à l' curried
infusion herbal tea
ingrédients ingredients

Jj

jambon ham
    jambon de Bayonne smoked cured ham
    jambon blanc (slice of boiled) ham
    jambon de Parme Parma ham
    jambon fumé (désossé) gammon
    jambon poché boiled ham
    jambon de York York ham (British-style)
jardinière garnished with spring vegetables
jarret knuckle

jauned'oeuf egg yolk
julienne julienne *[cut into fine strips]*
jus juice *[of meat, fruit]*
    au jus served in its own juices
jus (de fruits) (fruit) juice
    jus de citron lemon juice
    jus de fruits fruit juice
    jusd'orange orange juice
    jus de pomme apple juice
    jus de tomate tomato juice

French-English

Kk

kaki date plum, kaki
kasher *[casher]* kosher
kébab *[brochette]* kebab
ketchup *[sauce tomate]* ketchup
kirsch cherry liqueur
kiwi kiwi fruit
kouign amman Breton rich puff pastry butter cake
koulibiac see **coulibiac**
kumquat kumquat

Li

lactose lactose
lait milk
    au lait entier full fat, whole milk
    avec (du) lait, au lait with milk
    sans lait without milk
    lait condensé condensed milk
    lait de beurre *[babeurre]* buttermilk
    lait de brebis ewe's milk
    lait de chèvre goat's milk
    lait de coco coconut milk
    lait de soja soya milk
    lait de vache cow's milk
    lait demi-écrémé semi-skimmed milk
    lait écrémé skimmed milk
    lait entier full-cream milk
laitance soft roe
laitier dairy
    produits laitiers dairy products
laitue *[salade]* lettuce
    laitue iceberg iceberg lettuce
    laitue romaine cos lettuce
langouste crawfish, spiny lobster
langoustine Dublin bay prawn
langue tongue
    langue de boeuf ox tongue

French-English

lapereau young rabbit
lapin rabbit
lard de poitrine streaky bacon
  lard fumé smoked bacon
lardons cubed pieces of bacon
lasagne lasagne
  lasagne végétarienne/aux légumes
  vegetarian lasagne
lavabo toilet
lavande lavender
leberwurst liver sausage
légume vegetable
  légumes à vapeur steamed vegetables
  légumes bouillis boiled vegetables
  légumes braisés braised vegetables
  légumes verts green vegetables,
  greens
  légumes variés assorted vegetables
  petits légumes baby vegetables
légumineuses pulses
lentille lentil
  lentilles de Puy Puy lentils *[green or
  brown]*
letchi lychee
lieu jaune pollack
lieu noir saithe, coley
lièvre hare
limande dab
limande-sole lemon sole
lime *[citron vert]* lime
limonade *[citron pressé]* lemonade

lingue   ling
liqueur   liqueur
lisette   small mackerel
litchi   lychee
loganberry   loganberry
longe (de veau/porc/chevreuil)   loin (of
  veal/pork/venison)
lotte (d'eau douce)   burbot
    lotte de mer *[baudroie]* monkfish
loup   bass
    loup de mer   sea bass
lyonnaise   with sautéed onions
lyonnaise, sauce   sauce of onion, vinegar
  and brown stock

French-English

Mm

macaron macaroon
macaroni macaroni
macédoine de fruits fruit salad; fruit
  cocktail
    macédoine de légumes   mixed
    vegetables
mâche   lamb's lettuce
macis   mace
macrobiotique   macrobiotic
madeleine   small scallop-shaped sponge
  cake

madère *[vin]* Madeira

madère, sauce a demi-glace sauce with added Madeira and butter, served with ox tongue

maïs *[plant]* maize; *[US]* corn

    maïs (en épis/en grains) sweetcorn

    épi de maïs, maïs en épi corn on the cob *[sweetcorn]*

    farine de maïs cornmeal

    maïs soufflé popcorn

    semoule de maïs *[polenta]* polenta

maison home-made, of the house

    pâté maison home-made pâté

    maître d'hôtel, beurre butter mixed with lemon juice and chopped parsley, served with grilled meat or fish

malt malt

mandarine mandarin

mange-touts mangetout, sugar snap peas

mangouste, mangoustan mangosteen

mangue mango

maquereau mackerel

    maquereau mariné au vin blanc mackerel marinated in white wine

marc grape brandy

marcassin young boar

marchand de vin, sauce a sauce of red wine, shallots and stock

marché market

margarine margarine

mariné(e) marinated

French-English

marjolaine   marjoram
marmelade   (orange) marmalade
marmite   thick stew or soup; pot
marquise   rich frozen dessert of fruit or
  chocolate
marron   sweet chestnut
    marrons glacés   candied chestnuts
    purée de marron   chestnut purée
marsala   Marsala wine
massepain   marzipan
matelote   fish stew
mauvais(e)   bad
mayonnaise   mayonnaise
méchoui   North African spit-roasted lamb
méchouia   North African mixed vegetable
  salad
médaillon   medallion *[round piece of
  meat or fish]*
mélanger   to blend; to mix
mélasse   treacle
mélisse   lemon balm
melon   melon
menthe   mint
    menthe poivrée   peppermint
    menthe verte   garden mint
menu   menu
    menu à prix fixe   set menu
    menu du jour   today's menu
    menu enfants   children's menu
    menu gastronomique   gourmet menu
    menu touristique   mid-price menu

French-English

71

merguez North African spicy beef or lamb sausage
meringue meringue
merlan whiting
merlu *[colin]* hake
mérou grouper
mesclun Provençal salad of rocket, lamb's lettuce, endive
meunière, à la coated in flour and fried in butter
meurette Burgundy fish stew in red wine
mi-cuit(e) parboiled
miel honey
  rayon de miel honeycomb
mijoter to simmer
milanaise *[pasta]* with parmesan, tomato sauce; *[escalope]* breaded
millefeuille millefeuille, cream slice made with puff pastry
minestrone minestrone (soup)
mirabelle (small) yellow plum
mode, à la with ice cream
moelle bone marrow
mollusque mollusc
Mont Blanc dessert of chestnut puree with whipped cream
morilles morels *[mushrooms]*
Mornay with white sauce and cheese

morue cod

mouclade mussel stew with white wine, onion, cream and egg yolks

moudre to grind

moule mussel

    moules marinière moules marinière *[cooked with white Wine,onions,parsley]*

moulin à poivre pepper mill

moulu(e) ground (pepper, etc.)

mousse (de poisson, etc.) (fish, etc.) mousse

    mousse au chocolat chocolate mousse

mousseline mousse; purée

mousseline, sauce hollandaise sauce mixed with whipped double cream

moutarde mustard

    moutarde de Meaux whole grain mustard

mouton mutton

muffin muffin

mulet gris grey mullet

mûr(e) ripe

mûre (de ronce) blackberry

mûre (du mûrier) mulberry

myrtille blueberry, billberry, whortleberry

Nn

nage, à la   (fish) served in its stock
Nantua with crayfish
Nantua, sauce béchamel sauce with
  cream and crayfish butter
nappe tablecloth
nappé de   coated with *[sauce etc.]*
nature plain (yoghurt, etc.); (tea, coffee)
  without milk
navarin lamb stew
navet   turnip
navet   swede
nèfle medlar
nem   Vietnamese spring roll
niçoise, à la with olive oil, garlic,
  tomatoes, black olives
noisette hazlenut, cobnut
noisette *[de viande]* noisette *[small round*
  piece of fillet or loin]
noix nut; walnut
    noix d'acajou, noix de cajou   cashew nut
    noix de coco   coconut
    noix de coco séchée   desiccated
    coconut
    noix muscade   nutmeg
    noix de pécan, noix de pacane   pecan nut
    noix du Brésil   Brazil nut

noix du noyer blanc d'Amérique hickory nut

noix du noyer de Queensland macadamia nuts

noix de veau   tender cut of veal

non fumeurs *[section]* non-smoking (area)

nonnette   spiced bun

normande, à la   with cream, Calvados or cider

normande, sauce   a fish sauce with cream, egg yolks and butter

nougat blanc de Montélimar   white nougat made with honey and roasted almonds

nougatine brittle

nouilles noodles

Oo

oeuf   egg

   oeuf à la coque   soft-boiled egg

   oeuf dur   hard-boiled egg

   oeuf mollet   soft-boiled egg

   oeuf poché   poached egg

   oeuf pourri   bad egg

oeuf sur le plat   fried egg
oeufs à la neige *[île flottante]* floating islands *[dessert of poached egg whites in custard]*
oeufs et bacon, oeufs au bacon bacon and eggs
oeufs brouillés   scrambled eggs
oeufs de cailles   quail's eggs
oeufs de poisson   hard roe
oie goose
oignon   onion
olive olive
olives farcies   stuffed olives
olives noires black olives
olives vertes green olives
omble chevalier char *[fish]*
omelette omelette
omelette au fromage   cheese omelette
omelette au jambon   ham omelette
omelette aux épinards   spinach omelette
omelette aux fines herbs   herb omelette
omelette aux truffes   truffle omelette
omelette baveuse   omelette which is runny on top
omelette nature   plain omelette
omelette norvégienne   baked Alaska
onglet   flank of beef

French-English

orange   orange
  à l'orange   with orange
orge barley
    orge perlée   pearl barley
origan   oregano
ormeau   abalone
ortie nettle
os   bone
    os à moelle marrow bone
    (viande) avec l'os   meat on the bone
oseille   sorrel
oursin   sea urchin
ouvre-bouteille   bottle opener

Pp

paillasson de pommes de terre   grated
  sautéeed potato
paille au fromage   cheese straw
pain   bread
    pain à la farine de maïs   corn bread
    pain au chocolat rectangular
    croissant-style pastry with
    chocolate filling
    pain aux noix   walnut bread
    pain aux raisins   round croissant-style
    pastry with raisins

pain blanc white loaf, white bread
pain bis brown bread
pain complet wholemeal bread
pain croustillant crisp bread
pain de campagne farmhouse loaf
pain d'épice(s) gingerbread
pain de mie white sandwich loaf
pain de seigle rye bread
pain de son wholemeal bread
pain de viande meat loaf
pain grec *[sans levain]* pitta bread
pain grillé *[rôtie]* toast
pain moulé pan loaf
pain noir de Westphalie
pumpernickel bread
pain perdu French toast
palmier large crisp biscuit of flaky pastry
palourde clam
pamplemousse grapefruit
  jus de pamplemousse grapefruit juice
panaché *[boisson]* shandy
panaché de mixed plate of
panaché de légumes selection of
  vegetables, mixed vegetables
panais parsnip
pan bagnat Provençal hollowed-out roll
  filled with tomatoes, green peppers,
  olives, onions, anchovies
pané(e) breaded
papaye papaya, pawpaw
paprika paprika

parfait parfait
    parfait au café coffee parfait
Paris-Brest cake of chou pastry with
  praline filling
Parmentier with potatoes
parmesan Parmesan (cheese)
pastèque watermelon
pastis aniseed-flavoured aperitif mixed with
  water, particularly popular in the South
patate douce sweet potato; *[US]* yam
pâte pastry
    pâte à choux choux pastry
    pâte à frire batter
    pâte brisée shortcrust pastry
    pâte feuilletée puff pastry
pâte *[on cheese]* rind
pâte d'amandes almond paste
pâté pâté
pâté de campagne coarse pork pâté
pâté de canard duck paté
pâté de foie gras liver pâté
pâté de soja tofu
pâté de gibier en croûte game pie
pâtes (alimentaires) pasta
    pâtes fraîches fresh pasta
paté en croute meat pie
pâté végétal vegetable pie
pâtisserie French pastry; cake
patte leg
    pattes de dinde/de poulet
  turkey/chicken drumsticks

paupiette   thin rolled stuffed piece of
  meat
  paupiette de boeuf   beef olive
  paupiette de veau   veal olive
pavé   square or rectangular piece of
  steak, cheese, etc.
paysanne   served with carrots, turnips,
  onions, celery, potatoes,
peau   skin, peel
  sans peau   peeled
pêche   peach
peler   to peel
pelure   peel
  sans pelure   peeled
perche d'eau douce   perch
perdreau   young partridge
perdrix   partridge
périgourdine, à la   with truffles, liver
  pâté
persil   parsley
  persil frisé   curly parsley
  persil plat   flat parsley
persillé(e)   garnished with chopped parsley
pétillant(e)   sparkling, fizzy
petit beurre   butter biscuit
petit déjeuner   breakfast
petit pain   (bread) roll, bap
  petit pain au lait   bun
  petit pain au seigle   rye bread roll
petits fours   petits fours *[small dessert or
  cake]*

petits pois   green peas, garden peas
　　**petits pois gourmands, pois mange-
　　tout**   mangetout, sugar snap peas
petit-suisse   cream cheese in a pot, eaten
　with sugar
petits gris   small dark brown snails
pets de nonne   deep-fried fritters often
　served hot with sugar
pichet   carafe
　　un pichet de rouge   a carafe of red
　　wine
pickles   pickles
pieds de porc   pig's trotters
pieds et paquets   Provençal stuffed
　parcels of sheep's tripe cooked with
　trotters, wine, herbs and tomatoes
pigeon   pigeon
pigeonneau   squab
pignon   pine nut
pilaf aux champignons   mushroom pilaff
pilchard *[grosse sardine]*   pilchard
piment doux *[poivron]* pepper, capsicum
　　piment fort, piment rouge   chilli, red
　　chilli, chilli pepper
　　piment (fort) **en poudre**   chilli powder
　　piment de la Jamaïque   allspice
pimprenelle   burnet
pintade   guinea fowl
piperade   peppers, onions, garlic and
　tomatoes with beaten eggs and
　sometines ham

French-English

piquant(e) hot *[strong]*
pissaladière Provençal tart with onions, olives, tomatoes,anchovies
pistache pistachio (nut)
pistou (basil) pesto
plaquemine *[kaki]* persimmon
plat dish
>**plat du jour** dish of the day
>**plat principal** main course; *[US]* entree

plateau à fromage, plateau de fromages cheese board
pleurote oyster mushroom
plie plaice
poché(e) poached
>**poché dans du lait** poached in milk

pocher to poach
pochouse Burgundian stew of freshwater fish in white wine
poêlé(e) pan-fried
point, à *[rose]* medium-rare
pointes d'asperges asparagus tips
poire pear
>**poires au vin de Bourgogne** pears poached in red wine

poireau leek
petits poireaux baby leeks
pois pea
petits pois green peas, garden peas
pois cassés split peas
pois chiche chickpea

pois gourmands, pois mange-tout, mangetouts   mangetout
poisson   fish
   poisson d'eau douce   freshwater fish, river fish
   poisson de mer   sea fish
   poisson frit   fried fish
   poisson fumé   smoked fish
   poisson plat   flat fish
   poisson volant   flying fish
poisson-chat *[silure]*   catfish
poitrine   breast
   poitrine d'agneau/de veau   breast of lamb/veal
   poitrine de boeuf   brisket of beef
poivrade, sauce   a mix of vegetables cooked with wine, vinegar, pepper, and demi-glace sauce
poivre   pepper *[spice]*
   moulin à poivre   pepper mill
   poivre de cayenne   cayenne pepper
   poivre en grains   whole pepper
   poivre moulu   ground pepper
   poivre noir/vert/blanc   black/green/white pepper
poivrière   pepper pot
poivron   pepper *[vegetable]*
   poivron farci   stuffed pepper
   poivron rouge *[piment doux]* red pepper
   poivron vert   green pepper

French-English

polenta [*semoule de maïs*] polenta
pomme [*fruit*] apple
    pomme au four baked apple
    purée de pommes apple puree
pomme (de terre) potato
    pomme de terre au four baked potato
    pommes (de terre) dauphine
    croquettes of mashed potatoes mixed
    with choux pastry
    pommes (de terre) dauphinoises
    sliced potatoes baked with milk, cream,
    eggs and seasoning
    pommes (de terre) duchesse
    duchesse potatoes [mashed and mixed
    with egg yolk, baked]
    pommes de terre à l'anglaise/à l'eau
    boiled potatoes
    pommes de terre aux amandes
    amandine potatoes
    pommes de terre nouvelles new
    potatoes
    pommes de terre sautées fried
    potoatoes
    pommes allumettes matchstick potatoes
    pommes chips (potato) crisps; [US]
    potato chips
    pommes frites (potato) chips; [US]
    French fries
    pommes mousseline puréed potatoes
    pommes purée mashed potatoes;
    [US] creamed potatoes

porc pork
porcelet suckling pig pot jug
pot au chocolat chocolate pot
pot au feu braised meat or poultry and
  vegetables, with the broth served
  separately
potage soup
   potage au cari   mulligatawny (soup)
   potage aux légumes   vegetable soup
   potage bonne femme   leek and potato
   soup
   potage St Germain   green pea soup
potée thick soup or stew of pork, ham,
  cabbage, beans and other vegetables
potiron *[citrouille]* pumpkin
pouding fruit or milk pudding
   pouding au riz *[cuit au four]* rice
   pudding
   pouding cabinet cabinet pudding
   pouding de Noël *[anglais]* Christmas
   pudding
poularde fattened chicken
poule boiling fowl
poulet chicken
   poulet à la Kiev chicken kiev
   poulet frit fried chicken
   poulet rôti roast chicken
poulpe octopus
pourboire tip, gratuity
pourpier purslane
poussin poussin

poutassou   blue whiting
pré-cuit(e)   par-boiled
présure   rennet
   sans présure   rennet-free
primeurs   new season's fruit/vegetables
prix   price
à prix fixe   set, fixed-price
profiteroles   profiteroles
propre   clean
provençale, à la   with tomatoes, garlic,
  olive oil, olives
prune   plum
   prune de Damas   damson
pruneau   (sec) prune
prunelle   sloe
   eau de vie de prunelle   sloe gin
purée   puree
   en purée   mashed (potatoes); stewed (fruit)
   purée de pois   mushy peas
   purée de pois cassés   pease-pudding
purée de pommes   apple puree, apple sauce
purée de pommes de terre, pommes purée
mashed potatoes; *[US]* creamed potatoes

Qq

quark *[fromage blanc]* quark
quatre-épices   allspice

quenelles *[de brochet, de poulet ou veau]*
  quenelles *[oval dumplings of pike, chicken or veal, poached]*
quetsche   dark red plum
queue de boeuf   oxtail
    soupe à la queue de boeuf oxtail soup
queues de langoustine *[scampi]* scampi
quiche quiche
    quiche lorraine   quiche lorraine
    quiche au saumon fumé   smoked salmon quiche

Rr

râble (de lapin/lièvre)   saddle (of rabbit/of hare)
radis   radish, radishes
rafraîchi(e)   chilled
rafraîchisseur *[à vin]* wine cooler
ragoût *[fricassée]* stew
    ragoût de boeuf *[potée]*   hotpot
    ragoût de mouton à l'irlandaise   Irish stew
raie   skate
raifort   horseradish
raifort, sauce   a mixture of grated horseradish, vinegar and whipped cream. Served with roast beef and smoked fish

French-English

raisin(s) *[de table]* grape(s)
    raisins de Corinthe currants
    raisins de Smyrne sultanas
    raisins sec raisins
ramequin ramekin
rance rancid
râpé(e) grated
rascasse scorpion fish
rassis(e) stale
ratatouille ratatouille
ravigote, sauce a vinaigrette made with oil and vinegar, egg yolk, capers, parsley, tarragon, chervil, chives, and onion
ravioli ravioli
recette recipe
réglisse liquorice
reine-claude greengage (plum)
relever to spice up
rémoulade, sauce mayonnaise with capers, gherkins, anchovy.Served with fried fish
repas meal
requin shark
rhubarbe rhubarb
rhum rum
rillettes shredded potted pork or goose
rillons fried pieces of crispy pork or goose
ris de veau sweetbreads
rissole rissole
riz rice

riz au blanc, riz à la chinoise boiled rice
riz au lait au four baked rice, rice pudding
riz Caroline long-grained rice
riz complet brown rice
riz indien basmati rice
riz pour risotto risotto rice
riz rond pudding rice
riz sauvage wild rice
Robert, sauce fried onion with stock, mustard, and castor sugar added. Served with fried pork chop
rognon kidney
    rognons à la (sauce) diable devilled kidneys
romaine *[laitue]* romaine lettuce, cos lettuce
romarin rosemary
romsteck rump steak
roquette rocket
rosbif roast beef
rôti roast
    rôti de boeuf *[rosbif]* roast beef
    rôti de porc roast pork
rôti(e) roasted
rôtie *[pain grillé]* toast
rôtir to roast
rouget barbet red mullet
rouille mayonnaise made of chillies, garlic, and olive oil

roulade stuffed rolled (meat etc.)
roux a mixture of fat and flour cooked together, used as the base for sauces
russe, à la served with sour cream, hard-boiled egg and beetroot
rye *[whisky de seigle]* rye whisky

Ss

sabayon zabaglione
sablé shortbread
saccharine saccharin
safran saffron
sagou sago
saignant(e) *[viande]* rare *[meat, steak]*
saindoux lard
Saint Germain with green peas
Saint-Pierre dory, John Dory
saisir to sear
salade salad; lettuce
>**salade au poulet** chicken salad
>**salade César** Caesar salad
>**salade composée** mixed salad *[containing vegetables, meat or eggs, fish etc.]*
>**salade de fruits** fruit salad

French-English

salade de pommes de terre potato salad

salade de tomate tomato salad

salade mixte lettuce and tomato salad

salade niçoise salad of tomatoes, hard-boiled eggs, olives, anchovies, green beans, capers, potatoes, lettuce, green pepper, cucumber and/or tuna

salade panachée mixed salad

salade tiède warm salad

salade verte green salad

salade Waldorf *[pommes, céleri, noix, avec mayonnaise]* Waldorf salad

sale dirty *[plate, tablecloth, etc.]*

salé(e) salted; salty

salir to dirty

salmis game bird served in rich wine sauce made with remains of bird

salsifis salsify

sandre pike-perch

sandwich sandwich

sandwich au fromage cheese sandwich

sandwich au jambon ham sandwich

sanglier boar

sardine sardine

sarrasin *[blé noir]* buckwheat

sarriette savoury *[herb]*

sauce *[jus de viande]* sauce; gravy

sauce *[mayonnaise; vinaigrette]* dressing
sauce   sauce
    sauce à l'aneth   dill sauce
    sauce à la crème   cream sauce
    sauce à la menthe (fraîche)   mint sauce
    sauce au beurre butter sauce
    sauce au chocolat   chocolate sauce
    sauce au pain   bread sauce
    sauce aux canneberges   cranberry sauce
    sauce bigarade   *[bitter]* orange sauce
    sauce blanche *[béchamel]* white sauce
    sauce béarnaise   béarnaise (sauce)
    sauce bordelaise   bordelaise (red wine) sauce
    sauce diable   devilled sauce
    sauce espagnole   brown sauce
    sauce hollandaise   hollandaise sauce
    sauce madère   Madeira sauce
    sauce Mornay   cheese sauce
    sauce soja   soy sauce, soya sauce
    sauce tartare   tartar(e) sauce
    sauce tomate   tomato sauce
saucisse   sausage
    saucisse de Toulouse   fat pork sausage
saucisson   French sausage (pre-cooked)
    saucisson italien   salami
sauge   sage
saumon   salmon

saumon fumé smoked salmon
darne de saumon salmon steak
sauté(e) sautéed
sauter à la chinoise to stir-fry
sautoir sauté pan
au sautoir sautéd
saxifrage saxifrage
scampi scampi
seau de glace bucket of ice
sec (sèche) dry
très sec very dry *[wine]*
séché(e) dried
seiche cuttlefish
seigle rye
sel salt
qui contient peu de sel low-salt (dish)
sel gemme rock salt
selle (d'agneau) saddle
semoule semolina
serpolet wild thyme
serveur waiter
serveuse waitress
service service
service compris service included
service non compris service not included
service à la discrétion du client service discretionary
serviette (de table) napkin, serviette
sésame sesame seed
silure *[poisson-chat]* catfish

French-English

sirop syrup
> **sirop d maïs** corn syrup
> **sirop d'érable** maple syrup

socca chickpea flour pancake

soja (fève de) soy bean, soya bean
> **sauce soja** soy sauce, soya sauce

sole Dover sole; sand sole

sommelier wine waiter

son (de blé) bran

sorbet sorbet

sorgho sorghum

Soubise, sauce béchamel sauce with onion purée, flavoured with nutmeg. Used for roast meats

soucoupe saucer

soufflé soufflé
> **soufflé au fromage** cheese soufflé
> **soufflé aux fraises** strawberry soufflé

soupe soup
> **soupe à la queue de boeuf** oxtail soup
> **soupe à l'oignon** onion soup
> **soupe au pistou** Provençal soup of vegetables, noodles, beans,basil
> **soupe aux légumes** vegetable soup
> **soupe aux pois (cassés)** pea soup *[with split peas]*
> **soupe de poisson(s)** fish soup
> **soupe de poulet** chicken soup

souris d'agneau knuckle-end of leg of lamb (on the bone)

French-English

spaghetti spaghetti
sprat *[harenguet]* sprat
steak steak
    steak au poivre pepper steak
    steak (et) frites steak and chips
    steak tartare raw minced fillet steak
    served with raw egg yolk,capers, onions
stoemp Belgian dish of mashed potato
  and chopped vegetables
stout [bière brune] stout
stroganoff de champignons mushroom
  stroganoff
strudel aux pommes apple strudel
succédané de lait *[en poudre]* coffee
  whitener
sucre sugar
    sucre de canne cane sugar
    sucre d'érable maple sugar
    sucre d'orge barley sugar
    sucre glace, sucre en poudre icing sugar
    sucre roux *[cassonade]* (soft) brown
    sugar
    sucre semoule caster sugar
    sucre vanillé vanilla sugar
sucré(e) sweet
suif *(de boeuf)* suet
supplément supplement
    supplément légumes €3 vegetables
    €3 extra
suprême de poulet *[blanc, filet]* chicken
  breast, breast of chicken

surgelé(e)   frozen
syllabub   *[sabayon]* syllabub

French-English

Tt

table   table
taboulé   tabouleh
tagliatelle   tagliatelle
  **tagliatelles aux champignons et à la
  crème**   creamy mushroom tagliatelle
tajine   North African stew simmered in
  conical earthenware dish
tamiser   to sift
tanche   tench
tangerine   tangerine
tapenade   paste made of black olives,
  capers, lemon, anchovies,olive oil
tapioca   tapioca
tartare   see **steak tartare**
tarte pie
  part de tarte   slice of pie
  tarte à l'oignon   onion tart
  tarte aux fruits   fruit tart
  tarte aux noix de pécan   pecan pie
  tarte aux pom mes   apple pie
  tarte Tatin   upside down apple pie
  *[apples covered with pastry served
  upside down]*

tartelette   (small) tart
>   **tartelette à la crème**   custard tart
>   **tartelette aux pommes**   apple tart

tartine   slice of bread and butter

tasse   cup
>   **tasse à café**   coffee cup
>   **tasse à thé**   tea cup
>   **tasse de café** cup of coffee
>   **tasse de chocolat**   cup of cocoa/hot chocolate
>   **tasse de thé**   cup of tea
>   **tasse et soucoupe**   cup and saucer

tendre *[viande]*   tender

terrine   terrine *[chopped fish, meat or vegetable loaf]*

thé tea
>   **thé(au) citron**   lemon tea
>   **thé au lait**   tea with milk
>   **thé de Chine**   China tea
>   **thé glacé**   iced tea
>   **thé japonais**   Japan tea
>   **thé nature**   tea without milk or sugar
>   **thé vert**   green tea

théière   teapot

thon   tuna, tunny
>   **thon blanc**   albacore (tuna)

thym   thyme

tian   Provençal gratin of fish or vegetables cooked in a shallow dish

tiède   warm, not hot or cold *[salad etc.]*

tilleul   lime
timbale   cup-shaped mould
   timbale de poisson   fisherman's pie
tire-bouchon   corkscrew
tisane   herbal tea
tofu *[pâté de soja]* tofu
toilettes   lavatory, toilet
tomate   tomato
   tomate-cerise   cherry tomato
   tomate oblongue/italienne   plum tomato
   tomates farcis   stuffed tomatoes
   tomates séchées *(au soleil)*   sun-dried tomatoes
topinambour   Jerusalem artichoke
torsade   twisted plait
tourin   cream of onion soup
tournedos   fillet steak
tournesol   sunflower
   graines de tournesol   sunflower seeds
   huile de tournesol   sunflower oil
tourte   tart or flan with puff pastry
tourteau *[crabe]* crab
tranche   slice
   tranche de jambon   slice of ham
   tranche de pain   slice of bread
   tranche napolitaine   Neapolitan ice cream
tranché(e)   sliced (bread, etc.)
travers de porc spare ribs
tremper   to dip

trévise *[chicorée rouge]* radicchio
tripes tripe
    tripes à la mode de Caen tripe cooked with vegetables and white wine, for 7 to 8 hours
trou normand glass of Calvados or other spirits between courses to clear the palate
truffade Auvergne dish of potatoes, bacon, cheese and garlic, eaten with sausages
truffe truffle
    truffé garnished with truffle
    truffe au chocolat chocolate truffle
truite trout
    truite arc-en-ciel rainbow trout
    truite de mer sea trout
    truite saumonée salmon trout
tuile aux amandes thin almond biscuit similar to brandy snap
turbot turbot

French-English

Vv

vacherin meringue filled with ice cream or cream
vaisselle *[service de porcelaine]* china (service)
vanille vanilla

extrait de vanille vanilla essence
glace à la vanille vanilla ice cream
vapeur steamed
veau *[animal]* calf
veau *[viande]* veal
   escalope de veau veal escalope
   foie de veau calf's liver
   noix de veau tender cut of veal
végétalien (-ienne) vegan
végétarien (-ienne) vegetarian
velouté (de) cream (of) *[soup]*
   velouté de champignons cream of
   mushroom soup
velouté, sauce a white sauce made from
  fat and flour cooked till
lightly coloured, with added white stock
venaison venison
vermicelle vermicelli
verre glass
   verre à eau glass for water
   verre à vin wine glass
   verre d'eau glass of water
   verre de vin glass of wine
   verre propre clean glass
verte, sauce mayonnaise mixed with
  tarragon or chervil, chives
and watercress
verveine lemon verbena
viande meat
   viande de cheval horse meat
   viande en cocotte pot roast

viande froide cold meat
viande fumé smoked meat
vichyssoise vichyssoise *[leek and cream soup]*
viennoiserie croissants, brioches, pains aux raisins, etc
vigneronne, à la served with grapes and a wine sauce
vin wine
    vin blanc white wine
    vin corsé full-bodied wine
    vin de Bordeaux Bordeaux wine
    vin de Bourgogne Burgundy wine
    vin de pays local wine of a particular grape variety and area
    vin de Porto port
    vin de table table wine
    vin doux, vin de dessert dessert wine, sweet wine
    vin léger light-bodied wine
    vin local local wine
    vin (de la) maison house wine
    vin mousseux; vin pétillant sparkling wine
    vin rosé rosé(wine)
    vin rouge red wine
    vin sec dry wine
vinaigre vinegar
    vinaigre balsamique balsamic vinegar
    vinaigre de cidre cider vinegar
    vinaigre de vin (rouge/blanc) (red/white) wine vinegar

French-English

vinaigrette   French dressing, vinaigrette
vivaneau   red snapper
volaille   fowl; chicken
vol-au-vent   *[bouchée feuilletée; timbale]*
   vol au vent

WwZz

waterzooi   Belgian dish of chicken cooked
   in stock, white wine and cream with
   vegetables
WC   toilet, lavatory
whiskey irlandais   Irish whiskey
whisky écossais   whisky
xérès   sherry
yaourt   yoghurt
   yaourt à la grecque   Greek yoghurt
   yaourt nature   plain yoghurt
   yaourt aux myrtilles   blueberry
   yoghurt
yoghourt   yoghurt
zabaglione   zabaglione
zeste *[écorce râpée]* zest
   zeste de citron   lemon zest, grated
   lemon peel

English-French

Aa

abalone ormeau
absinthe absinthe
account compte
aïloli sauce ailloli,aïoli
air-conditioned climatisé(e)
albacore (tuna) thon blanc, germon
ale bière (anglaise) blonde; *see also* **beer**
alfalfa sprouts germes de luzerne
allergic allergique (à/au/aux...)
allergy allergie (à/au/aux...)
allspice piment de la Jamaïque
almond amande douce
   almond paste pâte d'amandes
   with almonds aux amandes
amandine potatoes pommes de terre aux amandes
anchovy anchois
   anchovy butter beurre d'anchois
   anchovy paste purée, pâte d'anchois
angel (food) cake angel cake *[génoise sans jaune d'oeufs]*
angel fish ange de mer
angel hair pasta cheveux d'ange
angels on horseback angels on horseback *[huîtres entourées de bacon, grillées, sur toast]*

angelica angélique
angler baudroie, lotte (de mer)
aniseed anis
aperitif apéritif
appetizer *[US]* *[drink]* apéritif;
    [food] amuse-gueule; hors-d'oeuvres
     apple pomme *[fruit]*
     apple fritter beignet de pommes
     apple juice jus de pomme
     apple pie tarte aux pommes
     apple puree purée de pommes
     apple sauce purée de pommes *[peu sucrée]*
     apple strudel strudel aux pommes
     apple turnover chausson aux pommes
     apple tart tartelette aux pommes
apricot abricot
aroma arôme; bouquet *[of wine]*
arrowroot arrow-root
artichoke artichaut
ashtray cendrier
asparagus asperge
    asparagus tips pointes d'asperges
aspic aspic
assorted vegetables choix de légumes, légumes variés
aubergine aubergine
au gratin *[US]* gratiné(e), au gratin
avocado avocat

Bb

baby   petit
    baby corn (cob)   tout petit épi de maïs
    baby leeks   petits poireaux
    baby vegetables   petits légumes
bacon   bacon, lard fumé
    bacon and eggs   oeufs au bacon
bad   mauvais(e)
    bad egg   oeuf pourri
bake   (faire) cuire au four
baked   cuit(e) au four
    baked Alaska   omelette norvégienne
    baked apple   pomme au four
    baked beans   haricots blancs aux
tomates; fèves au lard
    baked custard   flan
    baked potato   pomme de terre au four
    baked rice   riz au lait au four, pouding
au riz
bakery   boulangerie; *[for cakes]* patisserie
  balsamic vinegar   vinaigre balsamique
  banana   banane
    banana fritter   beignet de bananes
    banana split banana split *[banane,
glace à la vanille, Chantilly,amandes]*
    banana flambé   banane flambée
Barbary duck canard de Barbarie

barbecue barbecue
barbecued grillé(e) au barbecue
barbel rouget barbet **barley** orge
    barley sugar sucre d'orge
    barley water sirop d'orgeat *[fait avec de l'orge]*
basil basilic
    basil pesto pistou
basmati rice riz indien, riz Caroline
bass loup (de mer), bar
batons *[of carrots,etc.]* bâtonnets
batter pâte à frire
Bavarian cream bavarois
bay leaf feuille de laurier
bean haricot
    bean sprouts germes de soja
    broad beans grosses fèves; fèves des marais
    French beans, green beans, string beans haricot verts
    kidney beans haricots rouges
    runner beans haricots grimpants
    soya bean (fève de) soja
béarnaise (sauce) sauce béarnaise
  béchamel (sauce) (sauce) béchamel
  beech nuts faînes
beef boeuf
    beefsteak *[US]* bifteck, steak
    beef stock bouillon de boeuf
    beef Wellington filet de boeuf en croûte

English-French

English-French

  roast beef rosbif
beer bière
  draught beer bière (àla) pression
 beetroot betterave
bergamot bergamote
bib *[child's]* bavette, bavoir
bilberry airelle, myrtille
bill addition
biscuits biscuits, gâteaux secs
bitter amer (amère)
bitter bière anglaise pression
black butter beurre noir
black beans haricots noirs
blackberry mûre (de ronce)
black cherry cerise noire
black coffee café noir
blackcurrant cassis *[groseille noire]*
Black Forest cake/gateau forêt-noire
 black halibut flétan noir
black pepper poivre noir
black pudding boudin noir
blaeberry airelle, myrtille
blanch blanchir
blancmange blanc-manger
blend mélanger, incorporer
blinis blinis
blueberry myrtille, bleuet
blue cheese fromage bleu
blue whiting poutassou
boar sanglier; *[young]* marcassin

boil   (faire) bouillir

boiled   bouilli(e), cuit(e) à l'eau, à l'anglaise

   boiled egg   oeuf à la coque

   boiled ham   jambon poché

   boiled potatoes   pommes de terre à l'anglaise/à l'eau

   boiled rice   riz au blanc, riz à la chinoise

   hard-boiled egg   oeuf dur

bombe   bombe

bone   os

   boned   désossé(e) *[viande, poisson]*

   on the bone   *[meat]* avec l'os; *[fish]* dont les arêtes n'ont pas été retirées

   bones (of fish)   arêtes (de poisson)

bonito   bonite

borage   bourrache

bordelaise sauce   sauce bordelaise

borlotti beans   haricots italiens

bouquet garni   bouquet garni

bottle   bouteille

bottle opener   ouvre-bouteille

bowl   bol

brains   cervelle (de veau)

braise   braiser

braised   braisé(e)

bran   son (de blé)

brandy   cognac

cherry brandy cherry brandy, liqueur de cerise

brawn fromage de tête

Brazil nut noix du Brésil bread pain

breadcrumbs chapelure

bread knife petit couteau *[pour beurrer son pain]*

bread sauce sauce au pain

breaded pané(e)

breakfast petit déjeuner

bream brème (de mer)

breast poitrine

breast of lamb/veal poitrine d'agneau/de veau

chicken breast suprême de poulet

brill barbue

brioche brioche

brisket (of beef) poitrine (de boeuf)

brittle nougatine

broad bean grosse fève; fève des marais

broccoli (chou) brocoli

broth bouillon

brown *[verb]* (faire) brunir; (faire) dorer

brown bread pain complet

brown butter beurre noisette

brown rice riz complet

brown sugar sucre roux, cassonade

brown sauce sauce espagnole

Brussels sprouts choux de Bruxelles

bubble and squeak choux et pommes de terre frits

buckwheat sarrasin, blé noir
buffet buffet
bulgar wheat, bulgur wheat blé concassé
bun petit pain au lait
burbot lotte (d'eau douce)
burdock glouteron, bardane
burgundy (wine) (vin de) bourgogne; *see also* wine
burnet pimprenelle
burnt brûlé(e)
butcher's shop boucherie
butter beurre
>**butter sauce** sauce au beurre
>**with butter** avec beurre, au beurre
>**without butter** sans beurre
>**butterfish** blennie
>**buttermilk** lait de beurre, babeurre

Cc

cabbage chou
cabinet pudding pouding cabinet
Caesar salad salade César
caffeine caféine
>**caffeine-free** sans caféine, décaféiné(e)
cake gâteau

carrot cake   gâteau aux carottes
   cream cake   gâteau à la crème
   fruit cake   cake *[auxfruits confits]*
   sponge cake   génoise
calf   veau
   calf's brains   cervelle de veau
   calf's liver   foie de veau
camomile   camomille
canapés   canapés
candied   confit(e)
   candied peel   zeste confit, écorce confite
   candle   chandelle
candlestick   chandelier
candy *[US]* bonbon
cane sugar   sucre de canne
canned   en boîte (de conserve)
cantaloup (melon)   cantaloup
capers   câpres
capon   chapon
capsicum   piment doux, poivron
carafe   carafe
caramel   caramel
caraway (seeds)   cumin des prés, carvi
   carbohydrate   glucides *[hydrates de carbone]*
cardamom   cardamome
carp   carpe
carrot   carotte
   carrot cake   gâteau aux carottes
carve   découper

English-French

cassata cassate
cashew nut noix d'acajou/noix de cajou
  casserole casserole
caster sugar sucre semoule
catfish poisson-chat, silure
catsup *[US]* ketchup, sauce tomate
cauliflower chou-fleur
    cauliflower cheese chou-fleur sauce
    Mornay, au gratin
chau-navent swede
caviar caviar
cayenne pepper poivre de cayenne
celeriac céleri-rave
celery céleri
cereal *[breakfast]* *céréales*
chair chaise
champagne champagne
chantilly (crème) Chantilly
chanterelle chanterelle *[mushroom]*
char *[fish]* omble chevalier
charcoal charbon de bois
    charcoal-grilled grillé(e) au charbon
    de bois
chard bette,blette
charlotte charlotte
    apple charlotte charlotte aux
    pommes
    Cheddar (Cheese) (fromage) cheddar
    cheese fromage
    cheese board plateau à fromage;
    plateau de fromages

English-French

cheesecake gâteau au fromage blanc
cream cheese fromage à la crème
cheese sauce sauce Mornay
cheese soufflé soufflé au fromage
cheese straw paille, allumette au fromage
chef chef
cherry cerise
cherry brandy cherry brandy, liqueur de cerise
cherry tomato tomate-cerise
chervil cerfeuil
chestnut *[sweet]* marron, châtaigne
water chestnut châtaigne d'eau
chickpea pois chiche
chicken poulet
roast chicken poulet rôti
breast of chicken suprême de poulet
chicken gumbo (potage de) poulet et gombo
chicken Kiev poulet à la Kiev
chicken livers foies de poulets
chicken salad salade au poulet
chicken soup soupe de poulet
chicory endive
children's menu menu des enfants
chilled rafraîchi(e)
chilli piment fort, piment rouge
chilli con carne chili con carne
chilli pepper piment fort, piment rouge
chilli powder piment en poudre

china (service)   vaisselle; service de porcelaine
China tea thé de Chine
Chinese cabbage   chou de Chine
chipped *[glass, plate]* (verre, assiette) ébréché(e)
chips   (pommes) frites
chips *[US]* (pommes) chips
chitterling *[US]* friture de tripes *[découpées en morceaux]*
chives   ciboulette, civette
chocolate chocolat
   chocolate eclair   éclair au chocolat
   chocolate mousse   mousse au chocolat
   chocolate sauce   sauce au chocolat
   chocolate truffle   truffe au chocolat
chop *[cutlet]* côte, côtelette
chopped (into pieces)   en dés; (persil) haché
chopsticks   baguettes
choux pastry pâte à choux
chowder soupe de poisson à base de lait
   Christmas cake   gâteau de Noël *[anglais]*
Christmas log bûche de Noël
Christmas pudding pouding de Noël *[anglais]*
cider   cidre
   cider vinegar vinaigre de cidre
cinnamon   cannelle
citron   cédrat

citrus agrumes
clam clam, palourde
    clam chowder chowder aux palourdes
    claret bordeaux rouge
clean propre
clear up desservir (la table)
clear soup consommé
clementine clémentine
clove clou de girofle
    clove of garlic gousse d'ail
cobnut noisette
cockles coques
cocoa (poudre de) cacao
    cocoa butter beurre de cacao
    cup of cocoa une tasse de cacao/de
    chocolat
coconut noix de coco
    coconut milk lait de coco
    desiccated coconut noix de coco
    séchée cod morue, cabillaud
coffee café
    cappuccino coffee cappuccino
    coffee whitener succédané de lait *[en
    poudre]*
    coffee parfait parfait au café
    coffee pot cafetière
    coffee spoon cuillére à café
    decaffeinated café décaféiné, un déca
    espresso / expresso coffee café express
    filter coffee café filtre
    instant coffee café soluble

cold froid(e)
    cold cuts *[US]* assiette de viandes froides, assiette anglaise
    cold meat viande froide
coley *[coalfish]* lieu noir, colin
collared beef rosbif roulé *[ficelé]*
  condensed milk lait condensé
condiment condiment
confectioner's custard crème pâtissière
  conger eel congre, anguille de mer
  consommé (soup) consommé
    cold consommé consommé froid
  consommé en gelée
continental breakfast café complet
cook chef
cookies *[US]* biscuits, gâteaux secs
  coriander coriandre
corkscrew tire-bouchon
corn maïs
    corn bread pain à la farine de maïs
    cornflour fécule de maïs
    corn on the cob épi de mai's, maïs en épi
    corn syrup sirop de maïs
corned beef boeuf de conserve
cornet *[ice cream]* cornet (de glace)
cos lettuce (laitue) romaine
cottage cheese fromage 'cottage'
  courgette courgette
couscous couscous
crab crabe, tourteau, dormeur dressed
  crab crabe froid à l'anglaise/à/à la russe

English-French

prepared crab crabe décortiqué

crackling couenne croquante (du rôti de porc)

cranberry canneberge

cranberry sauce sauce de canneberges **crawfish** langouste

crayfish écrevisse

cream crème

double cream crème épaisse

single cream crème légère

whipped cream crème Chantilly, crème fouettée

cream cheese fromage à la crème

cream cake gâteau à la crème

cream sauce sauce à la crème *[béchamel]*

cream slice millefeuille *[où la crème Chantilly remplace la crème pâtissière]*

cream tea thé accompagné de scones avec confiture et crème fraîche

cream of crème (de), velouté (de)

cream of asparagus soup crème d'asperges

cream of chicken soup crème de volaille, velouté de volaille

cream of tomato soup crème de tomates

creamed en purée, à la crème

creamed potato *[US]* purée de pommes de terre

creamed spinach   purée d'épinards à la crème

creamy   en crème, crémeux(-euse), velouté(e)

crème caramel *[baked custard]* crème caramel

crème fraîche   crème fraîche

cress   cresson

crispbread   biscotte

crisps   (pommes) chips

croquette potatoes   croquettes de pommes de terre

croutons   croûtons

crumble   crumble

crumpet   petite crêpe épaisse *[non sucrée]*

  crystallised fruit   fruits confits

  cucumber   concombre

    cucumber sandwich   sandwich au concombre

cumin (seed)   cumin

cup   tasse

    cup and saucer tasse et soucoupe

    cup of coffee tasse de café; un café

    cup of tea tasse de thé; un thé

    coffee cup   tasse à café

    tea cup   tasse à thé

cured   fumé(e),mariné(e), salé(e)

currants   raisins de Corinthe

curry   curry, cari

custard   crème anglaise

    baked custard   flan

custard apple anone, pomme canelle
custard sauce crème anglaise
custard tart tartelette à la crème
cut couper
cutlery couvert
cutlet côtelette
cuttlefish seiche

English-French

Dd

dab limande
dairy products produits laitiers
damson prune de Damas
date datte
date plum kaki
debone désosser, lever les filets
decaffeinated, decaf (café) décaféine,
  un déca
deep-fried cuit(e) à grande friture
deer chevreuil
defrost dégeler
delicious délicieux (-euse)
demerara sugar sucre roux cristallisé
dessert dessert
dessert wine vin doux, vin de dessert
devilled (à la) diable

devilled kidneys rognons à la (sauce) diable

devilled sauce sauce (à la) diable

diced en cube

dill aneth

dill sauce sauce à l'aneth

dinner dîner

dip *[verb]* tremper

dip *[noun]* sauce froide *[pour crudités]*

 dirty *[adj]* sale

dirty *[verb]* salir

dish plat

dish of the day plat du jour

dogfish aiguillat, chien de mer done cuit(e)

under-done pas assez cuit(e); *[viande]* saignant(e) **well-done** bien cuit(e)

dory, John Dory Saint-Pierre, dorée

double cream crème épaisse

doughnut beignet

 jam doughnut beignet fourré à la confiture

Dover sole sole

draught beer bière (à la) pression

dressing vinaigrette

dried séché(e), sec (sèche)

sun-dried tomatoes tomates séchées (au soleil)

drink boisson

drinks included forfait boissons

drumsticks pattes de dinde ou de poulet

dry (wine) (vin) sec
Dublin bay prawn langoustine
duchesse potatoes pommes (de terre)
  duchesse
duck [*domestic*] canard (domestique)
    duck [*wild*] canard sauvage
    duck paté pâté de canard
    duck with oranges canard à l'orange
    duckling caneton, canette [*female*]
dumpling boulette de pâte
    potato dumpling gnocchi Parmentier

Ee

eclair éclair
eel anguille
egg oeuf
    boiled egg oeuf à la coque
    egg and bacon oeuf et bacon
    egg cup coquetier
    egg white blanc d'oeuf
    egg yolk jaune d'oeuf
    fried egg oeuf sur le plat
    hard-boiled egg oeuf dur
    omelette omelette
    poached egg oeuf poché
    scrambled eggs oeufs brouillés

soft-boiled egg   oeuf mollet
eggplant *[US]* aubergine
elderberry   baiedesureau
endive   chicorée frisée
entree *[starter]*entrée
entree *[US main course]* plat principal
escalope   escalope
    turkey escalope   escalope de dinde
    veal escalope   escalope de veau
    essence   extrait (de)
ewe's milk   lait de brebis
    ewe's milk cheese   fromage de (lait de) brebis

English-French

Ff

faggot ballottine
farm (eggs, chickens)   (oeufs, poulets) fermiers
fat *[adj]* gras (grasse)
fat *[noun]* gras
    fat-free   sans gras
fennel   fenouil
feta cheese   (fromage) feta, féta
fig figue
filbert   aveline
fillet filet

fillet steak tournedos, steak prélevé dans le filet
fillet of beef filet de boeuf
filleted désossé(e), en filets
filo pastry pâte phyllo
filter coffee café filtre
fine beans haricots verts (fins)
fish poisson
  anchovy anchois
  angel fish ange de mer
  bass loup (de mer), bar
  bream brème
  brill barbue
  burbot lotte (d'eau douce)
  catfish poisson-chat, silure
  cod morue, cabillaud
  coley *[coalfish]* colin, lieu noir
  conger eel congre, anguille de mer
  crayfish écrevisse
  cuttlefish seiche
  dogfish aiguillat, chien de mer
  dory, John Dory Saint-Pierre, dorée
  Dover sole sole *[la vraie]*
  eel anguille
  fish and chips friture de poisson avec frites
  fish stew matelote, bouillabaisse
  fish soup soupe de poissons
  fish cake croquette de poisson
  flounder flet
  flying fish poisson volant

grey mullet mulet gris
haddock aiglefin, églefin
hake merlu, colin
halibut flétan
herring hareng
kipper hareng saur/fumé
lemon sole limande-sole
mackerel maquereau
monkfish baudroie, lotte de mer
pike brochet
pike-perch sandre
pilchard pilchard, (grosse) sardine
red mullet rouget barbet
rockfish rascasse
roe oeufs de poisson, laitance
salmon saumon
scorpion fish rascasse
sea bass loup (de mer), bar
sea bream brème de mer
sea trout truite de mer, truite
saumonée
shark requin, aiguillat
skate raie
skipjack bonite
smelt éperlan
sole sole
sturgeon esturgeon
swordfish espadon
tench tanche
trout truite
tunny, tuna thon

turbot turbot
whitebait *[sprats]* blanchaille
whiting merlan
fisherman's pie timbale de poisson
fish shop poissonerie
fizzy pétillant(e), gazeux(-euse)
flageolet (beans) flageolet
flakes flocons
flambé flambé(e)
flan flan
flat fish poisson plat
flavour *[of ice cream]* parfum
flavoured aromatisé
floating island(s) oeufs à la neige, île(s)
  flottante(s)
flounder flet
flour farine
flying fish poisson volant
fondant fondant
fondue fondue
fool mousse faite de fruits, crème
  anglaise et Chantilly
fork fourchette
fowl volaille
    boiling fowl poule
free-range (egg, chicken) (oeuf, poulet)
  fermier

French beans   haricots verts
French dressing   vinaigrette
French fries *[US]* (pommes) frites
French toast pain perdu, pain doré
fresh   frais (fraîche)
freshwater (fish)   (poisson) d'eau douce
fried   frit(e)
fried chicken   poulet frit
fried egg   oeuf sur le plat
fried fish   poisson frit
    mixed fried fish   friture de poissons
    frisée (salad)   chicorée frisée
fritter   beignet
    apple fritter beignet de pommes
frog's legs   cuisses de grenouilles
frozen   surgelé(e)
fruit   fruit
    fruit cocktail   salade de fruits,
    macédoine de fruits
    fruit juice   jus de fruits
    fruit salad   salade de fruits,
    macédoine de fruits
fry   frire
fudge   fondant au chocolat
full-bodied wine   vin corsé
full-cream milk lait entier
full-fat (cheese)   (fromage) de lait entier

English-French

Gg

galantine   galantine
game   gibier (à plume, à poil); chevreuil
   game pie   pâté de gibier en croûte
   gammon   jambon fumé (désossé)
garden mint   menthe verte
garden peas   petits pois frais
garlic   ail
garlicky   aillé(e)
gateau   gâteau
gazpacho   gaspacho
gelatine   gélatine
ghee   beurre clarifié *[cuisine indienne]*
gherkin   cornichon
giblets   abats
gin   genièvre
ginger   gingembre
   ginger beer   bière au gingembre
   gingerbread   pain d'épice(s)
   ginger cake   gâteau au gingembre
glacé cherry   cerise confite
glass   verre
   clean glass   verre propre
   glass of water   verre d'eau
   wine glass   verre à vin
glazed   glacé(e)
gluten-free   sans gluten

GM *[genetically modified]* génétiquement modifié

goat chèvre

    goat's cheese fromage de chèvre

    goat's milk lait de chèvre

goose oie

    goose liver foie d'oie

gooseberry groseille à maquereau

goulash goulash, goulasch

granary loaf pain complet

granita granité

granulated sugar sucre granulé

grape(s) raisin(s) (de table)

grapefruit pamplemousse

grapeseed oil huile de pépins de raisin

grated râpé(e)

gratuity pourboire

gravy sauce, jus de viande

    gravy boat saucière

Greek yoghurt yaourt à la grecque *[au lait de brebis]*

green beans haricots verts

green olives olives vertes

green peas petits pois

green pepper poivron vert

green salad salade verte

greengage (plum) reine-claude

Greenland halibut flétan noir

greens légumes verts

grenadine grenadine

grey mullet mulet gris

grill *[verb]* griller, cuire sur le gril
grill *[noun]* gril
    mixed grill assiette de viandes grillées (assorties)
grilled grillé(e)
grind moudre
gristle cartilage, croquant
grits *[US]* bouillie de maïs, gruau de maïs
groats gruau d'avoine
grocery épicerie; *[small]* alimentation
  ground *[coffee]* moulu(e), *[meat]* haché(e)
    ground beef hachis, boeuf haché
groundnut oil huile d'arachide
grouper mérou
grouse grouse
guava goyave
gudgeon goujon guinea fowl pintade
gumbo gombo
gurnard grondin

Hh

haddock aiglefin, églefin
haggis haggis *[estomac de mouton contenant un hachis d'abattis de mouton, oignons et avoine, le tout bouilli]*
hake merlu, colin

half bottle demi-bouteille
halibut flétan
ham jambon
    boiled ham jambon poché
    slice of ham tranche de jambon
hamburger hamburger
hard-boiled egg oeuf dur
hard cheese fromage à pâte dure
hard roe oeufs de poisson
hare lièvre
haricot beans haricots blancs
hash browns *[US]* pommes de terre en
  dés, avec oignons, sautées
haunch cuissot
hazelnut noisette, aveline
heart coeur
heat up chauffer, réchauffer
herbs fines herbes
herbal tea tisane, infusion
herring hareng
hickory nut noix du noyer blanc
  d'Amérique
hollandaise sauce sauce hollandaise
hominy grits *[US]* bouillie de maïs
honey miel
honeycomb rayon de miel, gaufre de miel
honeydew melon cavaillon
hors d'oeuvre hors d'oeuvre
horse mackerel chinchard
horsemeat viande de cheval, cheval
horseradish raifort

hot *[not cold]* chaud(e); *[strong]*
   piquant(e)
hot dog hot dog *[saucisse de Francfort
   dans un petit pain]*
hotpot ragoût (de boeuf), potée

ice glace
   bucket of ice seau de glace *[pour
   garder le vin frais]*
ice cream glace, crème glacée
   ice cream cone cornet de glace/de
   crème glacée
   ice cream scoop boule de glace/de
   crème glacée
ice cube glaçon
ice lolly Esquimau®
iceberg lettuce laitue
iceberg icing glace, glaçage
   icing sugar sucre glace/en poudre
ingredients ingrédients, éléments
instant coffee café soluble
Irish stew ragoût de mouton à
   l'irlandaise
Irish whiskey whiskey irlandais

Jj

jam confiture
jelly *[savoury]* aspic, chaud-froid, galantine
jelly *[sweet/pudding]* gelée
jelly *[US, jam]* confiture
jello *[US]* gelée *[parfumée à la fraise, etc.]*
Jerusalem artichoke topinambour
John Dory Saint-Pierre, dorée
jug pot
jugged hare civet de lièvre
juice jus (de fruits; de viande)
julienne julienne

Kk

kaki kaki, plaquemine
kale chou vert frisé *[non pommé]*
kebab kébab, brochette (de viande)
kedgeree riz au poisson fumé avec oeufs durs et cari
ketchup ketchup

key lime pie tarte à la crème de citron vert
kidney rognon
kidney beans haricots rouges
king prawn crevette rose
kipper hareng fumé, hareng saur
kiwi fruit kiwi
knife couteau
knuckle jarret
kohlrabi chou-rave
kosher casher, kasher
kumquat kumquat

English–French

Ll

lactose lactose
  lactose intolerance intolérance au
  lactose
ladies fingers gombos
lager bière blonde
  a lager shandy un demi panaché
lamb agneau
  lamb chop côtelette d'agneau
lamb's lettuce mâche
langoustine langoustine
lard saindoux
lark alouette

lasagne   lasagne
latte (coffee)   café crème
lavatory   toilettes, WC, lavabo
lavender   lavande
leek   poireau
leg   patte
   leg of lamb   gigot d'agneau
legumes   légumineuses
lemon   citron
   lemon balm   mélisse
   lemon grass   citronnelle
   lemon juice   jus de citron
   lemon sole   limande-sole
   lemon zest   zeste, écorce de citron
   lemonade   limonade; *[freshly squeezed]* citron pressé
lentil   lentille
lettuce   laitue, salade
lime   citron vert, lime
ling   lingue
light-bodied wine   vin léger
liqueur   liqueur
liquorice   réglisse
liver   foie
   liver sausage   leberwurst
loaf   pain
   meat loaf   pain de viande
   white loaf   pain blanc, pain de mie
lobster   homard
   lobster bisque   bisque de homard

loganberry loganberry
loin (of veal/pork/venison) longe (de veau/porc/chevreuil)
low-fat *[diet]* basses calories; *[yoghurt etc.]* allégé
low in fat qui contient peu de gras; basses calories
low-salt qui contient peu de sel; hyposodé(e)
lunch déjeuner, lunch
luncheon meat viande froide pressée *[de conserve]*
lychee litchi, letchi

Mm

macadamia nuts noix du noyer de Queensland
macaroni macaroni
macaroon macaron
mace macis
mackerel maquereau
macrobiotic macrobiotique
Madeira madère
    Madeira cake génoise au citron, gâteau de Savoie

Madeira sauce   sauce madère
maize   maïs
mallard   colvert
malt   malt
mandarin   mandarine
mangetout   pois gourmands, pois mange-
  tout, mangetouts
mango   mangue
mangosteen   mangouste, mangoustan
maple syrup   sirop d'érable
maple sugar   sucre d'érable
margarine   margarine
marinated   mariné(e)
marjoram   marjolaine
market   marché
marmalade   marmelade d'oranges,
  confiture d'oranges
marrow *[vegetable]*   courge
marrow bone   os à moelle
    bone marrow   moelle
Marsala wine   marsala
marshmallow   guimauve
marzipan   massepain
mashed   en purée
mashed potatoes   pommes purée
matches   allumettes
matchstick potatoes   pommes allumettes
mayonnaise   mayonnaise
mead   hydromel
meal   repas **meat**   viande
    meat ball   boulette de viande

English-French

meat loaf   terrine/pain de viande
meat pie   tourte/pie de viande
medallion   médaillon
medlar   nèfle
melon   melon
melted butter   beurre fondu
menu   menu, carte
set menu   menu à prix fixe
meringue   meringue
milk   lait
cow's milk   lait de vache
ewe's milk   lait de brebis
goat's milk   lait de chèvre
soya milk   lait de soja
milk chocolate   chocolat au lait
poached in milk   poché dans du lait
with milk   avec (du) lait; au lait
without milk   sans lait
minced meat   hachis, viande hachée
mincemeat   mincemeat *[préparation sucrée à base d'un mélange de fruits et raisins secs, et de suif]*
mince pie   mince pie *[tarte(lette) avec mincemeat]*
mineral water   eau minérale
fizzy mineral water   eau gazeuse
still mineral water   eau plate
minestrone (soup)   (soupe) minestrone
mint   menthe
mint sauce   sauce à la menthe (fraîche)

English-French

mint jelly   gelée à la menthe
mixed grill   assiette de viandes grillées (assorties)
mixed salad   salade composée
mixed vegetables   macédoine de légumes
mollusc   mollusque
monkfish   baudroie, lotte de mer
morels   morilles
mousse   mousse, mousseline
muesli   müesli
muffin *[sweet, savoury]*   muffin
mug   mug, tasse *[sans soucoupe]*
mulberry   mûre *[du mûrier]*
mullet   rouget
mulligatawny (soup)   potage au cari
mushroom   champignon
  button mushrooms   champignons de Paris
mushy peas   purée de pois
mussel   moule
mustard   moutarde
mutton   mouton

English-French

Nn

napkin   serviette (de table)
natural   nature

Neapolitan ice cream tranche napolitaine
neat sans eau ni glace
nectarine brugnon, nectarine
nettle ortie
no smoking défense de fumer
non-smoking area section non fumeurs
noodles nouilles
nut noix
    almond amande
    Brazil nut noix du Brésil
    cashew nut noix d'acajou, noix de cajou
    chestnut marron
    cobnut noisette
    coconut noix de coco
    hazelnut noisette, aveline
    peanut arachide, cacah(o)uète
    pecan nut noix de pécan, noix de pacane
    sweet chestnut châtaigne, marron
    walnut noix
nutmeg noix de muscade

Oo

oatcake biscuit à la farine d'avoine *[pour manger avec le fromage]*

oatmeal   farine d'avoine
oats   avoine
   porridge oats   flocons d'avoine
octopus   poulpe
oil   huile
okra   gombo
olive olive
   black olives   olives noires
   green olives   olives vertes
olive oil   huile d'olive
omelette   omelette
on the rocks *[with ice]*   avec glace, on the rocks
onion   oignon
   onion soup   soupe à l'oignon
orange   orange
   orange juice   jus d'orange
   orange sauce   sauce à l'orange; *[less sweet]* sauce bigarade
oregano   origan
organic   biologique
ostrich   autruche
oven   four
overdone   trop cuit(e)
oxtail   queue de boeuf
   oxtail soup   soupe à la queue de boeuf
ox tongue   langue de boeuf
oyster   huître
oyster mushroom   pleurote

English-French

Pp

pancake   crêpe
pan-fried   à la poêle, poêlé(e)
papaya   papaye
paprika   paprika
par-boiled   pré-cuit(e), mi-cuit(e)
parfait   parfait
Parma ham   jambon de Parme
Parmesan (cheese)   parmesan
parsley   persil
    curly parsley   persil frisé
    flat parsley   persil plat
    parsley sauce   sauce au persil
    [béchamel fortement persillée]
parsnip   panais
partridge   perdrix; *[young]* perdreau
pasta   pâtes (alimentaires)
    fresh pasta   pâtes fraîches
pastry   pâtisserie
    filo pastry   pâte phyllo
    puff pastry   pâte feuilletée
    shortcrust pastry   pâte brisée
pasty   chausson avec viande et pommes
  de terre
pâté   pâté
    liver pâté   pâté de foie gras

pawpaw papaye
pea pois
    green peas petits pois
    green pea soup potage St Germain
    split peas pois cassés
    pea soup [with split peas] soupe aux pois (cassés)
peach pêche
peanut arachide
    peanut butter beurre de cacahouètes/d'arachides
pear poire
pearl barley orge perlée
pease-pudding purée de pois cassés
pecan nut noix de pécan, noix de pacane
    pecan pie tarte aux noix de pécan
peel [verb] peler, éplucher
peel [noun] pelure, peau, écorce
    grated peel zeste, écorce râpée
peeled sans pelure, sans peau
pepper [spice] poivre
    black/green/white pepper poivre noir/vert/blanc
    ground pepper poivre moulu
    whole pepper poivre en grains
    pepper mill moulin à poivre
    pepper pot poivrière
    pepper steak steak au poivre
pepper [vegetable] poivron
    green pepper poivron vert

English-French

red pepper poivron rouge

stuffed pepper poivron farci

peppermint menthe poivrée

perch perche (d'eau douce)

perry cidre de poire

persimmon plaquemine, kaki

pesto pistou

petits fours petits fours

pheasant faisan

pickled cabbage choucroute

pickled gherkin/cucumber cornichon (saumuré/au vinaigre)

pickled herring hareng mariné

pickled onion oignon au vinaigre

pickles pickles

pie tarte, tourte

pig porc, cochon

suck(l)ing pig cochon de lait, porcelet

pigeon pigeon

pig's trotters pieds de porc

pike brochet

pike-perch sandre

pilchard pilchard, (grosse) sardine

pineapple ananas

pistachio (nut) pistache

pitcher pichet, carafe

pitta bread pain grec *[sans levain]*

plaice plie, carrelet

plain nature

plantain banane verte *[à cuire]*

plate assiette
plum prune
plum pudding plum pudding, pouding de
Noël
plum tomato tomate oblongue, tomate
allongée
poach pocher
poached poché(e)
poached egg oeufpoché
polenta polenta, semoule de maïs
pollack lieu
pomegranate grenade
popcorn *(sweet/salted)* maïs soufflé
(sucré/salé)
porcini mushroom cèpe
pork porc
    pork chop côte de porc
    pork crackling couenne croquante (du
rôti de porc)
porridge porridge, bouillie d'avoine
port (vin de) porto
pot roast viande en cocotte
potato pomme de terre
    baked potato pomme de terre au four
    boiled potatoes pommes de terre à
l'anglaise
    fried potatoes pommes de terre sautées
    mashed potatoes purée de pommes
de terre, pommes purée
    new potatoes pommes de terre
nouvelles

English-French

146

potato chips   (pommes) frites
potato crisps   (pommes) chips
potato dumpling   gnocchi
Parmentier
potato salad   salade de pommes de
terre
potted shrimp   petite terrine de crevettes
au beurre
poultry   volaille
pound cake   gâteau quatre-quarts
poussin   poussin
prawn   bouquet, crevette rose
   Dublin bay prawn   langoustine
preserves   conserves
price   prix
prime rib   côte de boeuf [première
qualité]
profiteroles   profiteroles
prune   pruneau (sec)
pudding [savoury] pouding
pudding [sweet] dessert, pouding,
pudding
pudding rice   riz rond
pudding wine   vin de dessert, vin doux
puff pastry   pâte feuilletée
pulses   légumineuses
pumpkin   potiron, citrouille
purslane   pourpier

Qq

quail caille
  quails' eggs oeufs de cailles
quark quark, fromage blanc
quiche quiche
  quiche lorraine quiche lorraine
quince coing
Quorn® aliment à base de protéines
  végétales

Rr

rabbit lapin; *[young]* lapereau
rack carré
  rack of lamb carré d'agneau
  rack of ribs carré (d'agneau, de porc)
radicchio trévise, chicorée rouge
radish/radishes radis
ragout ragoût

rainbow trout   truite arc-en-ciel
raisin   raisin sec
ramekin   ramequin
rancid   rance
rare *[steak, meat]* saignant(e)
raspberry   framboise
ravioli   ravioli
raw   cru(e)
recipe   recette
red cabbage   chou rouge
red chilli   piment fort, piment rouge
redcurrant   groseille rouge
     redcurrant jelly   gelée de groseilles
redfish   rascasse
red mullet   rouget barbet
red pepper   poivron rouge, piment doux
  rouge
red wine   vin rouge
reindeer   chevreuil
rhubarb   rhubarbe
ribs   côtes
     rack of ribs   carré (d'agneau, de porc)
     ribs of beef   côtes de boeuf,
     entrecôtes
     spare ribs   travers de porc, côtes levées
rice   riz
     long-grained rice   riz Caroline
     rice paper   papier de riz
     rice pudding   pouding au riz; riz au lait
     [cuit au four]

risotto rice   riz pour risotto [*riz rond du Piémont*]
wild rice   riz sauvage
rind [*cheese*] pâte
ripe   mûr(e)
rissole   rissole
river   rivière; [*fish*] d'eau douce
roast [*verb*]   rôtir
roast [noun] rôti de boeuf/porc etc
  roast beef   rôti de boeuf, rosbif
  roast chicken   poulet rôti
  roast pork   rôti de porc
roasted   rôti(e)
rock salt   sel gemme
rocket   roquette
rockfish   rascasse
roe   oeufs de poisson
  hard roe   oeufs de poisson
  soft roe   laitance
roll [*bread*] petit pain
rolled oats   flocons d'avoine
rollmop herring   rollmop, hareng roulé (mariné)
romaine (lettuce)   romaine
room temperature   chambré(e)
rosé (wine)   (vin) rosé
rosehip   fruit de l'églantier
rosemary romarin rum   rhum
  rum baba   baba au rhum
rump steak   romsteak

English-French

runner bean   haricot grimpant
rusk   biscotte *[pour bébé]*
rye   seigle
rye bread   pain de seigle, pumpernickel
rye whisky   rye *[whisky de seigle]*

Ss

saccharin   saccharine
saddle   râble (de lapin); selle (d'agneau)
safflower   carthame
saffron   safran
sage   sauge
sago   sagou
saithe   lieu noir
salad   salade
    green salad   salade verte
    mixed salad   salade composée, salade panachée
    salad dressing   vinaigrette
    salad cream   crème mayonnaise
    side salad   salade verte *[en accompagnement]*
salami   saucisson italien
salmon   saumon
    salmon steak   darne de saumon

salmon trout   truite de mer, truite saumonée
salsify   salsifis
salt   sel
   low-salt   hyposodé(e)
salted   salé(e), avec sel
sand sole   sole *[plus petite que la 'vraie sole']*
sandwich   sandwich
   cheese sandwich   sandwich au fromage
   ham sandwich   sandwich au jambon
sardine   sardine
sauce   sauce
   white sauce   (sauce) béchamel, sauce blanche
saucer   soucoupe
saury   balaou
sausage   saucisse
   liver sausage   leberwurst
   sausage roll   friand
sautéed   sauté(e), au sautoir
sauté pan   sautoir
saveloy   cervelas
savoury   entremets salé
savoy cabbage   chou vert frisé *[pommé]*
scallion *[US]*   ciboule, cive
scallop   coquille St Jacques
scalloped chicken *[US]*   poulet en sauce blanche, au four
scalloped potatoes *[US]*   gratin dauphinois

English-French

scampi queues de langoustine, scampi
scone *[UK]* scone *[petit pain qu'on mange avec confiture et crème]*
scorpion fish rascasse
Scotch à l'écossaise
> **Scotch broth** potage de mouton, légumes et orge
> **Scotch egg** oeuf en croquette *[oeuf (dur) enrobé de chair à saucisse, pané et frit]*

scrambled eggs oeufs brouillés
sea bass loup (de mer), bar
sea bream brème de mer
seafood fruits de mer
sear (faire) saisir
seasoning assaisonnement
sea trout truite de mer
seaweed algue
semi-skimmed milk lait demi-écrémé
semolina semoule
service service
> **service discretionary** service à la discrétion du client
> **service included** service compris
> **service not included** service non compris

serviette serviette (de table)
sesame seeds graines de sésame
shad alose
shallot échalote

shandy panaché
  a half of shandy un demi panaché
shark requin, aiguillat
sharp fort(e), acide
shellfish crustacé, coquillage, fruits de mer
shepherd's pie hachis Parmentier
sherbet sorbet, granité
sherry xérès
shiitake mushrooms champignons chinois (shiitake)
shop magasin
shortbread sablé
shortcrust (pastry) pâte brisée
shoulder épaule, palette
shrimp crevette (grise)
  shrimp cocktail crevettes mayonnaise
sift tamiser
silverside gîte à la noix
simmer (laisser) mijoter
single cream crème (légère)
sirloin aloyau, faux-filet
skate raie
skewer brochette
skimmed milk lait écrémé
skin peau, pelure
skipjack bonite
slice tranche
  slice of bread tranche de pain
  slice of pie part de tarte

English-French

154

slice of ham tranche de jambon
sliced tranché(e)
sloe prunelle
  sloe gin eau de vie de prunelle
smelt éperlan
smoked fumé(e)
  smoked bacon lard fumé
  smoked cheese fromage fumé
  smoked eel anguille fumée
  smoked fish poisson fumé
  smoked haddock aiglefin fumé
  smoked kipper hareng saur, hareng fumé
  smoked meat viande fumé
  smoked salmon saumon fumé
snack *[light meal]* repas léger; *[between meals]* casse-croûte
snail escargot
snipe bécassine
soda bread pain au bicarbonate de soude
soda water eau de seltz
soft-boiled egg oeuf à la coque
soft cheese fromage à pâte molle
soft drink boisson (gazeuse) non alcoolisée
soft roe laitance
sole sole
sorbet sorbet
sorghum sorgho
sorrel oseille

soufflé   soufflé
    cheese soufflé   soufflé au fromage
soup   soupe, potage
    soup spoon   cuillère à soupe
    broth   bouillon
    chowder   soupe de poisson et légumes à base de lait
    consommé   consommé
    fish stock   court-bouillon
    fish soup   soupe de poisson(s)
    mulligatawny   potage au cari
    onion soup   soupe à l'oignon
    vegetable soup   soupe de légumes; minestrone
    vichyssoise   vichyssoise
sour   aigre
    sour cream   crème aigre
    sweet and sour   aigre-doux (-douce)
soya bean   (fève de) soja
soya milk   lait de **soja**
soya sauce   sauce soja
spaghetti   spaghetti
spare ribs   travers de porc, côtes levées
sparkling   pétillant(e)
    sparkling water   eau gazeuse
    sparkling wine   vin mousseux, vin pétillant
spice   épice
spicy   épicé(e)
spinach   épinard

English-French

spiny lobster   langouste
sponge biscuits   biscuits à la cuillère
sponge cake   gâteau mousseline; génoise
spoon   cuillère, cuiller
sprat   sprat, harenguet, anchois de
   Norvège
spring greens   jeunes feuilles de choux,
   brocolis, etc.
spring onion   ciboule, cive
spring water   eau de source
sprouts (Brussels)   choux de Bruxelles
squab   pigeonneau
squash   courge
squid   calmar, encornet
stale   rassis(e)
starter   entrée
steak *[beef]*   bifteck, steak
steak and kidney pie   pie de bifteck et
   rognons
steak and kidney pudding   pouding de
   bifteck et rognons
steamed   (cuit) à la vapeur
stew *[meat]* fricassée, ragoût
   lamb stew   navarin
stewed   *[meat]* (en) fricassée; *[fruit]* en
   compote
   stewed fruit   compote de fruits, fruits
   en compote
   stewed steak   fricassée/ragoût de
   boeuf

Stilton   fromage stilton
stir-fry   sauter à la chinoise
stock   bouillon
   vegetable stock   bouillon de légumes
stout   stout *[bière brune]*
straight *[US]*   sans eau ni glace
strawberry   fraise
   strawberry jam   confiture de fraises
   strawberry shortcake   gâteau fourré
   aux fraises, recouvert de crème
   Chantilly
streaky bacon   lard de poitrine, poitrine
  fumée
strip steak   entrecôte
stuffed   farci(e), fourré(e)
   stuffed olives   olives farcies
stuffing   farce
sturgeon   esturgeon
suck(l)ing pig   cochon de lait, porcelet
suet   suif (de boeuf)
sugar   sucre
   caster sugar   sucre semoule
   granulated sugar   sucre granulé
   icing sugar   sucre en poudre, sucre
   glace
sugar snap peas   petit pois gourmands,
  pois mange-tout
sultanas   raisins de Smyrne
sundae   coupe glacée
sunflower   tournesol

English-French

sunflower oil   huile de tournesol
supper   dîner, souper
supplement   supplément
swede   navet (de Suède), rutabaga
sweet   sucré(e), doux (douce)
  sweet (wine)   (vin) doux, vin de dessert
  sweet chesnut   châtaigne, marron
  sweet potato   patate douce
  sweet trolley   desserts *[présentés sur une table roulante]*
sweet and sour   aigre-doux (-douce)
sweetbreads   ris de veau
sweetcorn   maïs (en épis, en grains)
sweetener *[artificial]*   édulcorant
swiss roll   (gâteau) roulé
swordfish   espadon
syllabub   syllabub, sabayon
syrup   sirop

Tt

table   table
  tablecloth   nappe
  tablespoon   cuillère à dessert

table wine   vin de table
tagliatelle   tagliatelle
tangerine   tangerine
tapioca   tapioca
tarragon   estragon
tart   tartelette
tartar sauce   sauce tartare
tea   thé
    afternoon tea   (le) thé de 5 heures
    beef tea   bouillon de boeuf
    cup of tea   tasse de thé
    green tea   thé vert
    herbal tea   tisane, infusion
    high tea   repas de 5 heures *[Ecosse et Nord de l'Angleterre]*
    iced tea   thé glacé
    lemon tea   thé (au) citron
    teacake   brioche *[coupée, grillée, avec beurre, servie avec du thé]*
    teaspoon   cuillère à thé
    tea with milk   thé au lait
    tea-time   heure du thé
    teapot   théière
tench   tanche
tender   tendre
tenderloin   filet (de boeuf, de porc)
terrine   terrine
thrush   grive
thyme   thym
tin   boîte de conserve

English-French

tinned en boîte (de conserve)
tip pourboire
toad in the hole saucisses couvertes de pâte *[au four]*
toast pain grillé
    French toast pain perdu, pain doré
toffee caramel (au beurre)
tofu tofu, pâté de soja
tomato tomate
    tomato juice jus de tomate
    tomato ketchup ketchup, sauce tomate
    tomato salad salade de tomate
    tomato sauce sauce (à la) tomate
tongue langue *[de boeuf]*
toothpick cure-dent(s)
tope milandre
tough *[meat]* dur(e)
treacle mélasse
    treacle tart tarte au sirop de maïs
trifle trifle *[génoise, fruits, Chantilly]*
trimmings accompagnement, garniture
tripe tripes, gras-double
trout truite
truffle truffe
    chocolate truffle *[sweet]* truffe (au chocolat)
    truffle butter beurre de truffes
tuna, tunny thon
turbot turbot
turkey dinde

roast turkey   dinde rôtie
turmeric   curcuma
turnip   navet
turnip tops   fanes de navet
turnover   chausson (aux pommes, etc.)

Uu

uncooked   cru(e); qui n'est pas cuit(e)
underdone   pas assez cuit(e)
unsalted butter   beurre sans sel
upside-down cake   gâteau renversé

Vv

vanilla   vanille
vanilla essence   extrait de vanille
[liquide]
vanilla ice cream   glace à la vanille
vanilla pod/bean   gousse de vanille
vanilla sugar   sucre vanillé
veal   veau

veal escalope escalope de veau
vegan végétalien (-ienne)
vegetable légume
  vegetable soup soupe de légumes;
  minestrone
vegetarian végétarien (-ienne)
venison venaison, chevreuil
vermicelli vermicelle
very dry *[wine]* très sec
Victoria sponge (cake) génoise
vinaigrette vinaigrette
vinegar vinaigre
vine leaves feuilles de vigne
virgin olive oil huile d'olive vierge
vol au vent vol-au-vent, bouchée
  feuilletée
    chicken vol au vent bouchée à la
    reine

Ww

wafer gaufrette
waffles gaufres
waiter garçon, serveur
waitress serveuse
Waldorf salad salade Waldorf (pommes,
  céleri, noix, avec mayonnaise)

walnut   noix; cerneau (de la noix)
warm   *[salad etc.]* tiède
water   eau
    bottled water   eau en bouteille
    fizzy water   eau gazeuse
    glass of water   verre d'eau
    iced water   eau glacée, très froide
    jug of water   carafe d'eau
    mineral water   eau minérale
    sparkling water   eau gazeuse
    spring water   eau de source
    still water   eau plate, eau non gazeuse
watercress   cresson de fontaine
watermelon   pastèque
well done   bien cuit(e)
Welsh rarebit/rabbit   pain avec fromage grillé
whale   baleine
wheat   blé
whelk   buccin
whipped cream   crème Chantilly, creme fouettée
whisky   whisky écossais
whitebait *[sprats]* blanchaille
white   blanc (blanche)
    white bread   pain de mie, pain blanc
    white meat   viande blanche
    white wine   vin blanc
whiting   merlan
whole grain mustard   moutarde de Meaux

English-French

wholemeal bread pain complet
whortleberry myrtille
wild rice riz sauvage
wild strawberry fraise des bois, fraise
  sauvage
wine vin
    bottle of wine bouteille de vin
    glass of wine verre de vin
    house wine vin (de la) maison
    local wine vin local, vin de pays
    red wine vin rouge
    sparkling wine vin mousseux, vin
    pétillant
    sweet/pudding wine vin doux, vin de
    dessert
    wine cooler rafraîchisseur *[à vin]*
    wine list carte des vins
    wine vinegar *[red, white]* vinaigre de
    vin (rouge, blanc)
    wine waiter sommelier
    white wine vinblanc
winkle bigorneau
woodcock bécasse

English-French

YyZz

yam   igname; *[US]* patate douce
yoghurt   yaourt, yogourt
   plain yoghurt   yaourt nature
Yorkshire pudding   yorkshire pudding
  [beignet de pâte frite, salé]
zabaglione   zabaglione, sabayon
zest   zeste
zucchini *[US]*   courgette

Wines and spirits

by John Doxat

Major French wine regions

Alsace

Producer of attractive, light white wines, mostly medium-dry, widely used as carafe wines in middle-range French restaurants. Alsace wines are not greatly appreciated overseas and thus remain comparatively inexpensive for their quality; they are well placed to compete with popular German varieties. Alsace wines are designated by grape - principally Sylvaner for lightest styles, the widespread and reliable Riesling for a large part of the total, and Gerwürtztraminer for slightly fruitier wines.

Bordeaux

Divided into a score of districts, and sub-divided into very many *communes* (parishes). The big district names are *Médoc*, St Emilion, Pomerol, Graves and Sauternes. Prices for the great reds (châteaux Pétrus, Mouton-Rothschild, etc.) or the finest sweet whites (especially the miraculous Yquem) have become stratospheric. Yet 'château' in itself means little and the classification of various rankings of châteaux is not easily understood. Some tiny vineyards are entitled to be called château, which has led to disputes about what have been dubbed 'phantom châteaux'. Visitors are advised, unless wine-wise, to stick to the simpler designations.

Bourgogne (Burgundy)

Topographically a large region, stretching from Chablis (on the east end of the Loire), noted for its steely dry whites, to Lyons. It is particularly associated with fairly powerful red wines and very dry whites, which tend to acidity except for the costlier styles. Almost to Bordeaux excesses, the prices for really top Burgundies have gone through the roof. For value, stick to simpler local wines.

Technically Burgundies, but often separately listed, are the Beaujolais wines. The young red Beaujolais (not necessarily the over-publicised *nouveau*) are delicious when mildly chilled. There are several rather neglected Beaujolais wines (Moulin-à-Vent, Morgon, St Amour, for instance) that improve for several years: they represent good value as a rule. The Mâconnais and Chalonnais also produce sound Burgundies (red and white) that are usually priced within reason.

Champagne

So important is Champagne that, alone of French wines, it carries no AC (*appellation contrôlée*): its name is sufficient guarantee. (It shares this distinction with the brandies Cognac and Armagnac.) Vintage Champagnes from the grandes marques - a limited number of 'great brands' - tend to be as expensive in France as in Britain. You can find unknown brands of high quality (often offshoots of grandes marques) at attractive prices, especially in the Champagne country itself. However, you need information to discover these, and there are true Champagnes for the home market that are doux (sweet) or demi-sec (medium sweet) but are pleasing to few non-French tastes. Champagne is very closely controlled as to region, quantities and grape types, and is made only by secondary fermentation in the bottle. Since 1993, it is prohibited (under EU law) to state that other wines are made by the 'champagne method' - even if they are.

Loire

Prolific producer of very reliable, if rarely great, white wines, notably Muscadet,

Sancerre, Anjou (its *rosé* is famous), Vouvray (sparkling and semi-sparkling), and Saumur (particularly its 'champagne styles'). Touraine makes excellent whites and also reds of some distinction - Bourgueil and Chinon. It used to be widely believed - a rumour put out by rivals? - that Loire wines 'did not travel': nonsense. They are a successful export.

Rhône

Continuation south of Burgundy. The Rhône is particularly associated with very robust reds, notably Châteauneuf-du-Pape, and also with Tavel, arguably the finest of all still rosé wines. Lirac rosé is nearly as good. Hermitage and Gigondas are names to respect for reds, whites and rosés. Rhône has well earned its modern reputation - no longer Burgundy's poorer brother. From the extreme south comes the newly 'smart' dessert *vin doux naturel*, ultrasweet *Muscat des Beaumes-de-Venise*, once despised by British wine-drinkers. There are fashions in wine just like anything else.

Minor regions

Bergerac

Attractive basic reds; also sweet Monbazillac, relished in France but not easily obtained outside: aged examples can be superb.

Cahors

Noted for its powerful *vin de pays* 'black wine', the darkest red made.

Corsica

Roughish wines of more antiquity than breeding, but by all means drink local reds - and try the wine-based aperitif Cap Corse - if visiting this remarkable island.

Gaillac

Little known; once celebrated for dessert wines.

Jura

Virtually unknown outside France. Try local speciality wines such as *vin jaune* if in the region.

Jurançon

Remote area; sound, unimportant white wines, sweet styles being the better.

Midi

Stretches from Marseilles to the Spanish border. Outstandingly prolific contributor to the 'EU wine lake' and producer of some 80 per cent of French *vins de table*, white and red. Sweet whites dominate, and there is major production of *vins doux naturels* (fortified sugary wines).

Paris

Yes, there is a vineyard - in Montmartre! Don't ask for a bottle: the tiny production is sold by auction, for charity, to rich collectors of curiosities.

Provence

Large wine region of immense antiquity. Many and varied *vins de pays* of little distinction. Best known for rosé, usually on the sweet side; all inexpensive and totally drinkable.

Savoy

Good enough table wines for local consumption. Best product of the region is delicious Chambéry vermouth: as an aperitif, do try the well distributed Chambéryzette, a unique vermouth with a hint of wild strawberries.

Spirits

The great French spirit is brandy. Cognac, commercially the leader, must come from the closely controlled region of that name. Of various quality designations, the commonest is VSOP (very special old pale): it will be a cognac worth drinking neat. Remember, *champagne* in a cognac connotation has absolutely no connection with the wine. It is a topographical term, with *grande champagne* being the most prestigious cognac area;*fine champagne* is a blend of brandy from the two top cognac sub-divisions. Armagnac has become better known lately outside France, and rightly so. As a brandy it has a much longer history than cognac: some connoisseurs rate old armagnac (the quality designations are roughly similar) above cognac.

Be cautious of French brandy without a cognac or armagnac title, regardless of how many meaningless 'stars' the label carries or even the magic word 'Napoleon' (which has no legal significance).

Little appreciated in Britain is the splendid 'apple brandy', Calvados, mainly associated with Normandy but also made in Brittany and the Marne. The best is *Calvados du Pays d'Auge*. Do taste well-aged Calvados, but avoid any suspiciously cheap.

Contrary to popular belief, true Calvados is not distilled from cider -but an inferior imitation is. French cider (cidre) is excellent.

Though most French proprietary aperitifs, like Dubonnet, are fairly low in alcohol, the extremely popular Pernod/Ricard pastis-style brands are highly spirituous. Eau-de-vie is the generic term for all spirits, but colloquially tends to refer to local, often rough, distillates. Exceptions are the better *alcools blancs* (white spirits), which are made from fresh fruits and not sweetened as crèmes are.

Wine

Glossary of French wine terms

Abricotine

Generic apricot liqueur: look for known brands.

alcool blanc

Spirit distilled from various fruits (not wine) such as plums and raspberries; not fruit-flavoured cordials.

Aligoté

Light dry Burgundy.

Alsace

See **Major French wine regions**, p122.

anis

Aniseed, much favoured in pastis (Ricard/Pernod) type aperitifs.

Anjou

See **Loire, Major French wine regions**, p123.

aperitif

Literally 'opener': any drink taken as an appetiser.

Appellation (d'origine) Contrôllée

or AC wine, whose label will give you a good deal of information, will usually be costlier - but not necessarily better - than one that is a VDQS 'designated (regional) wine of superior quality'. A newer, marginally lesser category is VQPRD: 'quality wine from a specified district'. Hundreds of wines bear AC descriptions: you require knowledge and/or a wine guide to find your way around. The intention of the AC laws was to protect consumers and ensure wine was not falsely labelled - and also to prevent over-production. Only wines of reasonable standards should achieve AC status: new ones (some rather suspect) are being regularly admitted to the list.

Armagnac
See **Spirits**, p125.

Barsac
Very sweet Sauternes of varying quality.

Basserau
A bit of an oddity: sparkling red Burgundy.

Beaumes-de-Venise
Well-known vin doux naturel; see **Provence**, **Minor regions**, p124.

Beaune
Famed red Burgundy; costly.

Bergerac

Sound red wine from south-west France.

Blanc de Blancs

White wine from white grapes alone. Sometimes confers extra quality but by no means always. White wine made from black grapes (the skins removed before fermentation) is Blanc de Noirs. Carries no special quality connotation in itself.

Bordeaux

See **Major French wine regions**, p122.

bouchonné

Corked (describes wine that has gone 'off' and smells musty, usually because of a faulty cork allowing in bacteria)

Bourgeuil

Reliable red Loire wine.

Bourgogne

Burgundy; *see* **Major French wine regions**, p122.

brut

Very dry; description particularly applicable to best sparkling wines.

brut sauvage

Dry to the point of displeasing acidness to most palates; very rare though a few good wines carry the description.

Cabernet

Noble grape, especially Cabernet-Sauvignon for excellent, if not absolutely top-grade, red wines.

Cacao

Cocoa; basis of a popular crème.

Calvados

See **Spirits**, p125.

cassis

Blackcurrant; notably in crème de cassis (*see* **kir**).

cave

Cellar.

Cépage

Indicates grape variety; e.g. Cépage Cabernet-Sauvignon.

Chablis

See **Burgundy, Major French wine regions**, p122.

Wine

chai

Ground-level storehouse, wholly employed in Cognac and sometimes in Bordeaux and other districts.

Champagne

See **Major French wine regions**, p123. Also note **Méthode Traditionnelle** below.

Chardonnay

Popular, now international grape variety producing dry to buttery white wines.

Château(x)

See **Bordeaux, Major French wine regions**, p122.

Châteaneuf-du-Pape

Best known of powerful Rhône red wines.

Chenin-blanc

Grape variety associated with many fine Loire wines.

Clairet

Unimportant Bordeaux wine, its distinction being probable origin of English word *claret*.

clos

Mainly a Burgundian term for a vineyard formerly (rarely now) enclosed by a wall.

Cognac

See **Spirits**, p125.

Corbières

Usually a sound south of France red wine.

côte

Indicates vineyard on a hillside; no quality connotation necessarily.

côteau(x)

Much the same as above.

crème

Many sweet, sometimes sickly, mildly alcoholic cordials with many local specialities. Nearer to true liqueurs are top makes of crème de menthe and crème de Grand Marnier (q.v.). Crème de cassis is mixed with white wine to produce kir, or with a sparkling white wine to produce kir royal.

Crémant

Sparkling wine with strong but rather brief effervescence.

cru

Literally 'growth'. Somewhat complicated and occasionally misleading term: e.g. *grand cru* may be only grower's estimation, *cru classé* just means the wine is officially recognised, but *grand cru classé* is most likely to be something special.

cuve close

Literally 'sealed vat'. Describes production of sparkling wines by bulk as opposed to individual bottle fermentation. Can produce satisfactory wines and certainly much superior to cheap carbonated styles.

cuvée

Should mean unblended wine from single vat, but *cuvée spéciale* may not be particularly special: only taste will tell.

demi-sec

Linguistically misleading, as it does not mean 'half-dry' but 'medium sweet'.

digestif

Liqueur or brandy drunk after a meal to aid digestion.

Domaine

Broadly, Burgundian equivalent to Bordeaux château.

doux

Very sweet.

eau-de-vie

Generic term for all distilled spirits but usually only applied in practice to roughish marc (q.v.) and the like.

Entre-deux-Mers

Undistinguished but fairly popular white Bordeaux.

frappé

Drink served with crushed ice; e.g. crème de menthe frappée.

Fleurie

One of several superior Beaujolais wines.

glacé

Drink chilled by immersion of bottle in ice or in refrigerator, as distinct from frappé above.

goût

Taste; also colloquial term in some regions for local eau-de-vie (q.v.).

Grand Marnier

Distinguished orange-flavoured liqueur. *See also* crème.

Haut

'High'. It indicates upper part of wine district, not necessarily the best, though

Haut-Médoc produces much better wines than other areas.

Hermitage

Several excellent Rhône red wines carry this title.

Izarra

Ancient Armagnac-based liqueur much favoured by its Basque originators.

Juliénas

Notable Beaujolais wine.

kir

Well-chilled dry white wine (should be Bourgogne Aligoté) plus a teaspoon of crème de cassis (q.v.). Made with champagne (or good dry sparkling wine) it is kir royal.

liqueur

From old liqueur de dessert, denoting postprandial digestive. Always very sweet. 'Liqueur' has become misused as indication of superior quality: to speak of 'liqueur cognac' is contradictory - yet some very fine true liqueurs are based on cognac.

Loire

See **Major French wine regions**, p123.

marc

Mostly coarse distillations from wine residue with strong local popularity. A few marcs ('mar') - de Champagne, de Bourgogne especially - have achieved a certain cult status.

marque

Brand or company name.

Méthode Traditionnelle

Since the labelling ban prohibiting the use of the term 'champagne method' for wines made outside the Champagne district, this term is used for superior sparkling wine made in the same way as champagne, by fermentation in bottle.

Meursault

Splendid white Burgundy for those who can afford it.

Minervoise

Respectable southern red wine: can be good value as are many such.

mise

As in *mise en bouteilles au château* ('château-bottled'), or ... *dans nos caves* ('in our cellars') and variations.

Wine

Montrachet

Very fine white Burgundy.

Moulin-à-Vent

One of the rather special Beaujolais wines.

Muscadet

Arguably the most popular light dry Loire white wine.

Muscat

Though used for some dry whites, this grape is mainly associated with succulent dessert-style wines.

Nouveau

New wine, for drinking fresh; particularly associated with now tiring vogue for Beaujolais Nouveau.

pastis

General term for powerful anis/liquorice aperitifs originally evolved to replace banned absinthe and particularly associated with Marseilles area through the great firm of Ricard.

pétillant

Gently, naturally effervescent.

Pineau

Unfermented grape juice lightly fortified with grape spirit; attractive aperitif widely made in France and under-appreciated abroad.

Pouilly-Fuissé

Dry white Burgundy (Macon); sometimes over-valued.

Pouilly-Fumé

Easily confused with above; a very dry fine Loire white.

porto

Port wine: usually lighter in France than the type preferred in Britain and popular, chilled, as an aperitif.

primeur

More or less the same as nouveau, but more often used for fine vintage wine sold en primeur for laying down to mature.

rosé

'Pink wine', best made by allowing temporary contact of juice and black grapes during fermentation; also by mixing red and white wine.

Wine

Sauvignon

Notable white grape; *see also* **Cabernet**.

sec

'Dry', but a wine so marked will be sweetish, even very sweet. Extra Sec may actually mean on the dry side.

sirop

Syrup; e.g. sugar-syrup used in mixed drinks, also some flavoured proprietary non-alcoholic cordials.

Supérieur(e)

Much the same as Haut (q.v.) except in VDQS.

VQRPD

See **Appellation (d'origlne) Contrôllée** above, p128.

vin de Xeres

Sherry ('vin de 'ereth').

Wine

French Cheeses

How can anybody be expected to govern a country that has 246 kinds of cheese?

(Charles de Gaulle)

France is one of the biggest cheese producers in the world. Since de Gaulle's original comment in 1962 the number of types of cheese it offers has grown to around 500.

French cheeses fall into six main categories:

- fresh cream cheeses such as petit-suisse

- surface-ripened soft cheeses such as Brie and Camembert

- washed-rind soft cheeses such as Pont l'Evêque

- goat's cheeses such as Crottin de Chavignol

- blue cheeses such as Roquefort and Bleu d'Auvergne

- cooked and uncooked pressed cheeses such as Comté and Reblochon, with a firm texture.

Cheese

Fresh cheeses are made from unpasteurised milk and do not undergo any ripening or fermentation process. Surface-ripened cheeses are allowed to ripen for a few weeks until a white mould, called a bloom, forms. Washed-rind cheeses are repeatedly washed in warm salt water to encourage a firm rind to form. Pressed cheeses are pressed in a mould for up to 12 months; in the case of cooked cheeses they are heated before being pressed.

Like the best French wines, the quality of French cheeses is tightly regulated and the top 40 carry the 'Appellation d'origine controlee' mark (AOC). This means that their origin and quality is strictly controlled and guarantees, among other things, that the cheese originates from a specific region of France and has been produced using traditional methods.

The criteria laid down for AOC cheeses are rigorous:

- The cheese has to come from a geographically precise area such as a municipality or a district. The milk must come from this particular region too and the cheese must be produced and partly matured there as well.

- The production methods have a strong influence on the characteristics of a cheese. In order to ensure top quality, AOC cheeses have to be made by strictly defined methods that have been handed down over centuries.

- The size, type of rind, texture and minimum fat content of the cheese are all responsible for its final flavour. These characteristics are precisely defined and have to be adhered to strictly by producers, who are inspected by Ministry of Agriculture staff responsible for monitoring the authenticity and quality of the products.

The current AOC cheeses are listed here, together with the type of milk used to make them and the area they originate from.

Cheese	Description	Origin
Abondance	hard cow's milk cheese produced from unpasteurised milk, with fruity nutty flavour	Haute Savoie (eastern France)

Cheese	Description	Origin
Beaufort	hard cow's milk cheese produced from unpasteurised milk, with fruity aromatic flavour	Savoie (eastern France)
Bleu d' Auvergne	semi-soft blue cheese from unpasteurised cow's milk, with full nutty flavour	Auvergne (central France)
Bleu de Gex	semi-soft cheese made from unpasteurised cow's milk, with a distinctive hazelnut flavour	Rhône-Alpes/Jura
Bleu des Causses	semi-soft blue cow's milk cheese stronger than Bleu d'Auvergne	Midi-Pyrénées

Cheese	Description	Origin
Bleu du Vercors	semi-soft blue cow's milk cheese, mild nutty flavour	Rhône-Alpes
Brie de Meaux	soft surface-ripened cheese from unpasteurised cow's milk, with mild fruity taste	Ile-de-France
Brie de Melun	like Brie de Meaux but with stronger smell	Ile-de-France
Brocciu	soft cream cheese made from unpasteurised sheep or goat's milk	Corsica
Camembert de Normandie	soft surface-ripened cheese from unpasteurised cow's milk	Normandy
Cantal	firm drum-shaped cheese	Auvergne

Cheese	Description	Origin
	from unpasteu rised cow's milk	
Chabichou du Poitou	soft cone-shaped cheese from unpaste urised goat's milk, with mild flavour	Poitou-Charente (west France)
Chaource	soft surface-ripened drum-shaped cow's milk cheese with delicate flavour	Champagne (north-east France)
Chevrotin	semi-soft cheese of unpas teurised goat's milk	Rhône-Alpes/
Comté	hard wheel-shaped cheese from unpaste urised cow's milk	Franche Comté
Crottin de Chavignol	soft goat's milk cheese in small cylinder shape, with acidic flavour	central France

Cheese	Description	Origin
Epoisses de Bourgogne	soft washed-rind cow's milk cheese with strong smell and rich, mildly alcoholic taste; sold boxed as it becomes runny as it ripens	Burgundy
Fourme d'Ambert	semi-soft blue cow's milk cheese, cylindrical, with tangy flavour	Auvergne
Fourme de Montbrison	semi-soft blue cow's milk cheese, cylindrical, milder than Fourme d'Ambert	Auvergne
Laguiole	semi-soft drum-shaped cheese made from unpasteurised cow's	southern Auvergne

Cheese	Description	Origin
	milk, with tangy flavour	
Langres	soft washed-rind cow's milk cheese that is sunken on top, a strong smell and a tangy flavour	Champagne/ Burgundy region
Livarot	soft cylindrical cow's milk cheese with washed rind and a pungent smell; ripens to a strong, spicy flavour; bound with leaves	Pays d'Auge (Normandy)
Maroilles	square soft cow's milk cheese with washed rind and a strong flavour	northern France

Cheese

Cheese	Description	Origin
Mont d'Or	soft unpasteurised cow's milk cheese with a buttery flavour, sold boxed; becomes runny as it ripens	Rhône-Alpes
Morbier	firm cheese from unpasteurised cow's milk, with distinctive dark stripe through the middle and a mild fruity flavour	Franche-Comté
Munster	soft unpasteurised cow's milk cheese with washed, strong-smelling rind; often eaten with caraway seeds	Alsace-Lorraine
Neufchâtel	semi-soft surface-ripen	Normandy

Cheese	Description	Origin
	ed heart-shaped cow's milk cheesex with slightly tangy taste	
Ossau-Iraty	round firm sheep's milk cheese with nutty flavour	Pyrénées
Pélardon	soft unpasteurised goat's milk cheese, often eaten baked	Languedoc-Roussillon
Picodon	soft disc-shaped goat's milk cheese with fresh acidic flavour, often grilled	Rhône-Alpes
Pouligny Saint-Pierre	soft cone-shaped goat's milk cheese with nutty flavour	central France

Cheese	Description	Origin
Pont l'Evêque	square soft cow's milk cheese with a washed rind that has a pungent aroma, and a mild flavour	Normandy
Reblochon	semi-soft cheese from unpasteurised cow's milk with creamy, fruity taste	Savoie
Rocadamour	soft cheese made from unpasteurised goat's milk with nutty, acidic taste	Midi-Pyrénées
Roquefort	semi-soft blue sheep's milk cheese with strong salty flavour	Midi-Pyrénées

Cheese

Cheese	Description	Origin
Saint-Nectaire	semi-soft cow's milk cheese with mild flavour	Auvergne
Saint-Maure de Touraine	log-shaped soft unpasteurised Touraine goat's milk cheese with grey rind and straw in centre	Touraine (central France)
Salers	firm cheese from unpasteurised cow's milk, similar to Cantal	Auvergne
Selles-sur-Cher	small round soft goat's milk cheese	Loire
Vacherin du haut Doubs	same as Mont d'Or	
Valençay	pyramid-shaped soft goat's milk cheese with ash-	central France

Cheese	Description	Origin
	covered rind and a mild nutty flavour	

Apart from the top 40 listed above, here are some other well-known French cheeses you are likely to encounter:

Cheese	Description	Origin
Cantadou	cow's milk cheese in small balls that can be used as a spread	non-regional
Caprice des Dieux	oval mild soft white cheese	Champagne-Ardennes
Chaumes	full-flavoured soft cow's milk cheese with washed rind and buttery flavour	Périgord
Coulom miers	a smaller Brie-type cheese	Ile-de-France

Cheese

Cheese	Description	Origin
Etorki	firm sheep's milk cheese	French Basque region
Le Pié d'Angloys	soft full-fat cow's milk cheese that ripens in its box	Burgundy
Mimolette	Edam-type cow's milk cheese, dark orange when mature	north-east France (originally Lille)
Port Salut	mild semi-soft cow's milk cheese	non-regional
Raclette	firm cow's milk cheese, often used in cooking as it melts easily	Auvergne
Saint Agur	semi-soft blue cow's milk cheese with mild creamy flavour	Auvergne

Cheese	Description	Origin
Saint Felicien	soft unpasteurised cow's milk cheese with fresh flavour	Burgundy
Saint Marcellin	soft round cow's milk cheese	Dauphine
Saint-Paulin	mild semi-soft cow's milk cheese	mainly Brittany and Normandy
Tomme (de Savoie)	firm unpasteurised cow's milk cheese with hard grey rind and creamy taste	Rhône-Alpes
Vignotte	semi-soft cow's milk cheese with a rich creamy flavour	Champagne

Cheese

V French cheeses for vegetarians

The French AOC mark generally implies that a cheese has been made with animal rennet, so vegetarians have to search further afield for cheeses that are suitable to eat. Look for commercial brands such as Boursin, Tartare and Saint-Morêt. Companies such as Milleret (who make le Gylois, le Charcennay, le Roucoulous and l'Ortolan), Rippoz (who make Emmenthal, Morbier, Raclette and Tendre), OMA, Guilloteau and Entremont all produce cheeses made with non-animal-based rennet.

Serving cheese

The French eat their cheese before, or in place of, the dessert course. Cheese can be eaten with bread, or sometimes just on its own, and should be served at room temperature.

Different cheeses go with different types of bread: for example a soft creamy cheese such as Neufchâtel or Chaource goes well with fruit or nut bread. Cheese connoisseurs in particular like to eat the rind, so do not remove it before serving. Some rinds however are more suitable for eating than others.

Cheese

Ideally a cheese should be divided up so that each p iece has some rind on it.

- Small round cheeses such as Camembert or some goat's cheeses can be cut into portions from the centre like cakes

- Square cheeses such as Pont 1'Evêque can also be cut diagonally, then each half sliced into smaller triangles

- Cheeses with a soft rind that have been cut from a larger 'wheel', such as Brie, are sliced starting from the narrowest point of the triangle

- Blue cheeses such as Roquefort are also cut into triangles, fanning out from the centre of the narrower end

- Firmer cheeses such as Comté are cut across in straight slices, with the thickest slice then cut into two so that each piece shares some rind

- Log-shaped cheeses — mainly goat's cheeses such as Sainte-Maure—are sliced across into rounds. The smaller,round, goat's cheeses should simply be cut into halves or thirds

- Divide pyramid- or cone-shaped cheeses such as Pouligny Saint-Pierre into vertical triangles starting from the middle, so they do not crumble

- Cheeses sold in boxes, such as Epoisses and Mont d'Or, can be eaten straight from the box with a spoon if they are sufficiently ripe.

Serving wine with cheese

As a general rule of thumb it is safe to assume that a cheese will go well with local wines from the same region. Another general guideline is that the stronger the cheese, the more full-bodied the wine should be to balance it. Heavy sweet white wines such as Sauternes go surprisingly well with a range of cheeses, including strong blue cheeses.

Soft surface-ripened cheeses such as Brie go well with light or medium-bodied reds such as Beaujolais or Médoc. Another good principle is to match washed-rind cheeses or firm cheeses such as Munster, Reblochon and Tomme with full-bodied reds such as Saint-Emilion or Chateâuneuf-du-Pape, or with white Alsace wines.

Cheese

Goat's cheeses can be accompanied by Sauvigon blanc or Chardonnay wines, or other dry and fruity white wines. Blue cheeses can either be partnered with a full-bodied red or — a famously successful combination — with a sweet white wine such as Sauternes.